Just Another
BOOK

Authorized King James Bible Inspired and Preserved

MICHAEL DUNN

xulon
PRESS

Copyright © 2013 by Michael Dunn

Just Another Book
Authorized King James Bible Inspired and Preserved

by Michael Dunn

Printed in the United States of America

ISBN 9781628710397

All rights reserved solely by the author. The author guarantees all contents are original and do not infringe upon the legal rights of any other person or work. No part of this book may be reproduced in any form without the permission of the author. The views expressed in this book are not necessarily those of the publisher.

Unless otherwise indicated, Bible quotations are taken from the King James version of the Bible. Copyright © 1769.

www.xulonpress.com

DEDICATION

I would like to dedicate this book to the transport driver that had the courage to share the Lord with an unsaved 19 year old summer student who was on his way to University in the fall. After sharing the Gospel message, Richard Tykolis gave me a copy of the Gospel of John (KJV) and said a simple prayer, "Lord open Michael's eyes and make yourself real to him". Six years later the Lord graciously answered this man's prayer as he led me to the Lord in the cab of his truck in 1973. I remain eternally grateful to this man and his wonderful wife Lois who spent so much of their time helping my wife and I to grow in the Lord in those formative years.

I especially have to dedicate this book to my wife, Lynda.

This book would have been impossible without the love and support of my soul mate. Lynda and I fell in love when we were just teenagers in High School and I knew early on in our relationship that this was the girl I was going to marry. We got married in my last year of University and we lived on a lot of macaroni and cheese. Financially, it was perhaps the most difficult year of our marriage but one that we often look back on today and have a good laugh.

Over the years when the storms of life raged around us and life became difficult, she was the one who was always there. She was the safe place I could go to share my heart and the soft place to lay my head when I needed understanding and comfort. She never lost faith in her husband and she continues to be the love of my life and my very best friend.

To say that the Lord has blessed our home and our lives would be an understatement. I remain eternally grateful to a loving compassionate Saviour who redeemed me from my sin and saved my soul. It is my desire and prayer that this book will bring honor to His name... For His name is Wonderful.

Acts 4:12
Neither is there salvation in any other: for there is none other name under heaven given among men, whereby we must be saved

TABLE OF CONTENTS

1. About the Author 7
2. Why Another Book on the Bible. 16
3. Inspiration / Preservation / Literal Interpretation 30
4. Textual Criticism of the Bible 55
5. The Authorized 1611 King James Bible 71
6. Other English Bibles and Translation Comparisons. . . 105
7. What Must I do to be Saved? 132
8. In Closing. 166

Chapter One

ABOUT THE AUTHOR

Have you ever wondered how a child who once believed in the Story of Creation; Adam and Eve; Noah and the Ark; Jonah and the Whale; David and Goliath; the Gospel Message; songs about the 'B I B L E yes that's the Book for me' and then they enter High School and go through what I believe to be a spiritual metamorphosis where their whole mindset on Biblical truths suddenly changes into doubts, fears and unbelief? How does this happen so quickly or should I say so easily and so often?

There is a problem within the Bible believing Christian community that I believe lies at the core of the issues facing our Church and especially our young people today. The very foundation upon which we have built our Church and our family has shifted. The absolutes upon which we trusted have been thrown under the bus and life as we once knew it has changed.

Before I get into these issues, I feel a need to tell you who I am. Many of you will be able to identify with my life because I am just like you. I am not a Preacher. I have never held the office of a Deacon or a Trustee, nor have I been on a Church Board. I am a layman and this book is being written from a layman's point of view.

I have filled the pulpit when my Preacher has been out of town and I have taught many Sunday School Classes over the years and led several people to the Lord, but I am not a spiritual giant. I still have my battles.

I was born in the town of Fort Erie, Ontario Canada on July 9, 1948. Back then Fort Erie was a tough little border town situated on the upper Niagara River just across from Buffalo New York and connected by the Peace Bridge. I got saved in 1973 when I was 25 yrs. old. I am an Anglican by birth; I married a Catholic; I was led to the Lord by a transport driver from a United Brethren in Christ Church of which I became a member. I am now a Baptist by choice. If there ever was an ecumenical movement, I guess I am one.

I am not ashamed to admit that I am a Born Again Christian, a Dispensationalist, a Pre- Millennialist and I read and study from the Cambridge Authorized King James Bible 1769 Edition.

Romans 1:16 – 17
16. For I am not ashamed of the gospel of Christ: for it is the power of God unto salvation to every one that believeth; to the Jew first, and also to the Greek.
17. For therein is the righteousness of God revealed from faith to faith: as it is written, The just shall live by faith.

I am a true Canadian with a mix of Irish, Scotch and English in my background. My mother (Dorothy Little) was born in New Liskard Ontario. Her mother was Irish, whose family came to Canada and settled in Buckingham Quebec. My mother's father was from Scotland. He died from double pneumonia when my mother was just a young girl and her mother (with 2 boys and 2 girls) moved to Timmins Ontario to live with her sister. Grandma Little met and re-married a tough ironworker named Rod Giguere. He would never let me call him Grandpa and insisted on Uncle Rod. He was one of the most rugged men I ever met. My mother, left Timmins and moved to Fort Erie when she was only 16 years old to work with her older sister Jean at Fleet Industries during WWII.

My father, Wray Dunn, was born in Fort Erie and came from a large family of 11 children; 3 boys and 8 girls. Although there was some English in his background, you better be ready to drop the gloves if you ever indicated to my father that we were anything but Irish. He was a rough Garrison Rd. country boy who loved to play baseball. He was on a Senior Men's Baseball team that was inducted into the Fort Erie Sports Hall of Fame and was a well-known pool shark and hustler at the local pool halls and hotels. He was a hard working truck driver who loved to drink, fight and chase women. How my mother ever met and fell in love with such a character goes beyond all sound reason. They got married when they were 19 years old and had five boys of which I am the second born. We were all raised, baptised, and confirmed in the Anglican Church, however, we only went as a family to weddings, funerals, and occasionally on Christmas Eve and Easter.

My mother was an Angel. How she ever put up with my father is a testimony of true grit and courage. But stay with him she did. Her whole reason for being was to raise her five boys. She was the best. We always had food on the table, a clean house, clean clothes, and a lunch to take to school and a mother to come home to. It was all about family with her. She was a very beautiful, stubborn, tough little lady who held the family together and loved her boys with a love that was so strong and unconditional that when I studied about the love of Christ for the sinner, I instantly thought of my mother. I have seen her standing in our driveway arguing with the police to leave her boys alone, while my brother and I were hiding in the bedroom guilty as sin. My father used to say if it wasn't for your mother we wouldn't have a pot to pee in or a window to throw it out. And that was the absolute truth. Go figure.

Although my Dad was a heavy drinker for most of his life, and although he was at times a very difficult man to live with, he was my Dad (me Da) and I loved him and he in turn loved me. He took me everywhere with him and I mean everywhere. All the boot-legers knew me and I knew them on a first name basis. When my Dad was sober, he was a great man to be around. He was a very kind and generous person who had a great deal of compassion for the down and outer. If I had a nickel for every dollar he gave to a person in need, I would be a rich man. He just could not control his drinking, and many a time I had to hitch-hike to the hotel late at night and drive him home. That started when I was about 12 or 13 years old and continued well into my late teens. He eventually stopped his heavy drinking, and the last 10 years of his life and his marriage to my mother were all good. He finished his life well. He proved to be a loving husband, a wonderful father and a loving caring Grandfather to my three boys.

After many years of praying for my parents, I had the privilege of leading my father to the Lord two months before he died of cancer in September 1997. That Christmas my mother asked me to take her to the grave side and it was there that she prayed with me to receive the Lord into her heart as her personal saviour. What an honour it was to lead both my father and my mother in the prayer of salvation. This is a vivid reminder that we serve a longsuffering, kind, tender, and compassionate Lord who is still in the business of answering our prayers.

I graduated from the University of Buffalo in 1972. I was the only one of five boys to get a University degree, and that was only possible because of a Hockey Scholarship. I got married to my wife, Lynda in 1971 during my last year of University. She is a beautiful French Canadian girl who lived just down the street. Her mother was born in Scotland, and her father was of French Canadian and Ojibway decent. I fell in love with Lynda in High School when she was only

15 years old. She became my best friend and my biggest fan. We went everywhere together; every baseball game, every lacrosse game, every hockey game, we were inseparable. After 41 years of marriage and three beautiful boys, she remains the love of my life and is still my biggest fan and my best friend.

I always said that when I got married it would be different. I would never treat my wife like my father treated my mother. Not so. I was more like my Dad than I care to admit. I was a weekend alcoholic, a drinker and a fighter and came close to losing my marriage. Then something wonderful happened; God saved me! I did a complete 180, and the Lord helped me to become the kind of man I had always wanted to be. The Lord saved my soul, saved my marriage and blessed us with three amazing boys. Our boys are the joy of our life and now Lynda and I have two grandchildren. I did not think I could love anyone as much as I love my boys, however, that was before Cherith and Cameron were born. Amidst all the pictures in our living room, my wife has a sign that says, 'All Because Two People Fell in Love'. To say we are blessed is an understatement.

It wasn't long before I discovered that the Christian life is not for sissies. It is a battle from start to finish. If you do not believe me then carry your Bible to work or to school and put it on your desk. Take it with you to the lunch room or to the cafeteria and openly read it as you sit there with your friends. The fact is that most of us are secret Christians who are completely intimidated by the world.

The Bible tells us that we are to put off the old man and put on the new man which is created in righteousness and true holiness. *(Ephesians 4:22-24)* This however, is easier said than done. Just when you think you have arrived that old man comes home and starts a fight with the new man and the rug gets pulled out from under you.

You have no idea how hard I prayed for my Dad when we found out he had cancer and for my Mom when she had major complications with her diabetes. The old man showed up a few times through the process of watching my parents die but the Lord gently carried me through and was very precious and close when I needed Him to hold me up.

My father died in my arms, and I held my mother's hand and kissed her forehead as she died from complications with her diabetes. Like my mother I have diabetes and like my father I went through a battle with cancer. There is nothing like having your doctor look you in the eyes and say "Mr. Dunn you have cancer." Believe me that sets you back! I went through a very serious operation to remove my prostate in 2006 and have been clear of cancer ever since. Praise the Lord.

In January 2008 after winning the most prestigious award that my company had; the President's Club Award; my boss tried to move me to the other side of Canada. When I refused to go, he forced the issue and the company let me go. I won the President's Club Award in 2005, was down with cancer for 3 months in 2006 and then won the Award again in 2007.

How does one win an award like that for the second time in three years, battle through cancer and then lose the highest paying job he ever had? At 60 years of age I certainly wasn't prepared for this. I felt violated and like a total reject. I had the love and support of my wife, my boys and many wonderful Christian friends, but I was embarrassed and in denial for a long time.

I poured my heart out to the Lord and stayed active in my Church. I continued to pray and read my Bible every day. It was through the Book of Psalms that the Lord ministered to my heart and this situation proved to be one of the greatest periods of spiritual growth in my life. He walked with me and at times had to carry me but He was always there. Jesus went above and beyond my expectations as He graciously met all of my needs. He is so good.

Deuteronomy 31: 8
And the LORD, he *it is* that doth go before thee; he will be with thee, he will not fail thee, neither forsake thee: fear not, neither be dismayed.

I became a Church hopper for a few years looking for the perfect Church. Guess what? There are no perfect Churches because there are no perfect people and if you are expecting your Preacher to keep you or your children spiritual and walking with the Lord, then guess what again? That is a responsibility that God has given to the parents and in particular to the father. Going to a Church with a good Preacher is important but raising your children is not your Preacher's job. Every one of us is a sinner in need of a Saviour and our walk with the Lord is our walk to walk. Our relationship with the Lord is a personal one. Having said that, I cannot over emphasize the importance of attending a good Bible Church. There is nothing that can compare to a good local Church family that helps to encourage you and your family in your walk with the Lord. It is critically important to fellowship with other likeminded believers. However, our walk with the Lord is a personal endeavour and something that no other person can do for you. It is your journey and God's desire is for you to develop a deep and personal relationship with Him along the way.

Hebrews 10:25
Not forsaking the assembling of ourselves together, as the manner of some *is;* but exhorting *one another:* and so much the more, as ye see the day approaching.

I got married in my last year of University while Lynda was working full time at a company called Horton CBI. When we decided to start a family, she quit work a couple of months after she discovered that she was pregnant. Her mother passed away when she was only 7 years old, and she was a latch-key kid all of her adolescent and teen life. My wife was adamant about being a stay at home Mom and raising her own children. She did work part time when the boys were all in school, but was home by the time the boys were let out of school. Our boys always came home to a Mom that was waiting for them with snacks and kisses.

We were a busy family as all our boys played travel hockey, baseball and lacrosse. We helped as much as we could to put them through University and College and had an unfinished basement for years because of the expenditures of giving ourselves to our children's needs.

Our boys are certainly not perfect and each one is a unique individual, with their own personality. They are so different and yet so much alike. They all grew up to be well adjusted hard working corporate citizens. We are a caring, loving, compassionate family that continues to share a lot of quality time together.

I have been blessed with the fellowship of many great men of God; Preachers, teachers, deacons and many wonderful people who helped me to grow in my faith. I have been saved for over 40 years and have attended several Churches in the process. I was saved in a United Brethren in Christ Church; this Church split and we became Golden Harvest Baptist Chapel. I then went to Bible Baptist Church in Niagara Falls and then Garden City Baptist Church in St. Catharines. I have since returned to Golden Harvest Baptist Church. Golden Harvest is a very good Church with a great Pastor from North Carolina, an ex-Vietnam veteran who loves the Lord and never fails to give an invitation for salvation every Sunday.

For several years now, I have been concerned about what we as Christians consider to be the 'Authority' upon which we are to build our lives. In the beginning this concern started out as just another one of my personal studies, however, it grew into something much bigger. This book is an effort to take you where the Lord took me; into the realm of Divine Inspiration and Divine Preservation of God's Word. This is not meant to be an in-depth presentation, however, I believe it is something that Christians need to hear and something that the Lord has laid on my heart to do.

Let me tell you what this book is not. It is not a personal vendetta on my part against any one Church or any one Preacher. This book will raise a lot of questions; questions that we will go through in the following chapters. The purpose of this book is to encourage you to go deeper than you ever have before and to… 'Study to shew thyself approved unto God, a workman that needeth not to be ashamed, rightly dividing the word of truth.' (*2 Timothy 2:15*)

If God uses this book to draw you closer to His Word and in the process closer to Him, then it has accomplished that for which it is designed to do.

If this book brings you to the saving knowledge of our wonderful Saviour then it has accomplished that which is the desire of our Lord's heart for you.

I trust that I have set the background on who I am and would like to close this opening chapter by saying this…… "If God can graciously save a sinner like Michael Dunn then His Grace is sufficient for you."

Unless otherwise noted, all the Scripture used in this book is taken from the Authorized King James Bible 1769 Edition.

Chapter Two

WHY ANOTHER BOOK ON THE BIBLE

Before I get into this book, I have to admit that I am 'Old School'. Over the years, I have seen some big time changes within our Fundamental (oh there's a bad word) Bible Churches. Many Churches have cancelled their Sunday Evening Service and/or their Wednesday Evening Prayer Meetings. For many Christians, it has even become a struggle to attend the Sunday morning service on a regular basis and in most Churches the adult Sunday School Classes are hit and miss. People no longer read their Bible on a consistent basis and very few actually study the Word. In fact, many no longer bring their Bibles to Church; but why should they? Now many churches have the overhead with the Bible verses for them; the congregation no longer stands together for the reading of Scripture before the preaching and very few preachers open their message with prayer.

Indifference has taken over in many Bible Churches. Families who once had a time of family devotion have stopped doing so, and many never take time to get alone with God and pray; that is until disaster strikes! Then all of a sudden it is "LORD WHAT ARE YOU DOING TO ME?" "LORD HELP ME!!" "LORD HEAL ME" "LORD GIVE ME"…ME…ME…ME.

When 911 hit in New York City, I know exactly where I was and who I was with. The world was in shock and the Churches were filled with people getting right and seeking the Lord. I have heard several testimonies about people who got saved as a direct result of 911. However this didn't last long. As soon as the dust settled, people went back to being themselves.

We have Churches full of 'Ho Hum Christians' with no desire to study the Bible; Ho Hum Preachers and Ho Hum Teachers, just going through the motions, no heart, no passion. People keep fidgeting in their seat looking at their watch; it has all become white noise to them.... yada yada yada....blaa blaa blaa.....come on Preacher....the football game starts at 1pm....I want to go fishing.....to go golfing.....to go visit the Grandkids. Going through the motions has become a Christian art form for many of us today. I have heard all the buzz words when sitting in Tim Horton's having a coffee with other Christians as we struggle to maintain our spiritual persona. Many Christians live on a superficial level suspended somewhere between the world and living for the Lord.

Here is a check list for you.

What ever happened to the old fashioned Altar Calls? If your Church still has an altar call, then when was the last time the Holy Spirit spoke to your heart of hearts during a message from the pulpit or from a Sunday School lesson and moved you to go forward and ask the Lord for forgiveness or to ask the Lord for the strength to overcome a weakness or to pray for a lost loved one?

What Book and Chapter did your Preacher preach from last Sunday? Did you take notes? Can you openly discuss how the preaching or teaching affected your life?

Do you have a set time to read your Bible and if so then what Book in your Bible are you currently studying through right now?

I must sound very self-righteous and maybe even a bit mean spirited at this point. Trust me, I go through all these struggles from time to time myself. The Christian life for me is a constant battle and from what I have seen over the last several years, the same can be said about many of my Christian friends. I believe the Church is at a cross-road and in fact I think it may be too late to turn her around. Just take a look at the attendance of your Sunday evening service, or your Wednesday evening prayer meeting (if you still have one) and this will tell you a lot about the state of your Church. In fact, several Churches in our area cancel their Sunday Evening Services and Wednesday Night Prayer Meeting during the summer vacation months?

As the family goes, so goes the Church and many Christian families are in a mess. Many of our teenage and adult (born-again) children are no longer attending Church. Children that we went the extra mile for, dedicating them to the Lord, taking them to Church, Sunday Morning, Sunday Evening, Wednesday Evening Prayer meeting and Awana, spending our time, energy and money on Christian School and/or 'Home Schooling'. Sacrifice after sacrifice and after all that, our children no longer have the desire to be in Church or to even associate with or be around other Christians. We have to beg them to come out for a Christmas or an Easter service. Our sons date and marry unsaved girls and our daughters date and marry unsaved boys and far too many of these relationships fall apart and end up in separation and/or divorce. We have to stop and give our heads a shake and ask ourselves the question..........what happened?

True Biblical Salvation should be a life changing event. Our Pastor is always reminding us that there should be a time, a place and a set of conditions that one can look back on to identify the day of our Salvation; a time and a place when we gave our heart and soul over to the Lord Jesus Christ and committed ourselves to walking with Him the rest of our days.

I sure remember October 9, 1971. I stood at the altar in St. Paul's Anglican Church and watched Lynda walk down the aisle with her father. Oh brother, she was radiant! I gave my heart to the girl that still remains the love of my life. My life was changed that day! Our marriage has had its moments but once we got saved, we learned to work through the hard times and our marriage became a 100% commitment to each other and our love grew and matured. We both knew that we were in this for the long haul and we were connected at the hip. We were one and God has blessed us beyond anything we could have imagined. If someone were to ask me if I was married, I wouldn't stand there and say I think so, or I sure hope so. I know so! I was there when it happened and this is how our relationship should be with the Lord. This should be an easy question to answer; when were you saved; where were you saved and what were the conditions of your salvation i.e. when, where and how did it take place?

Matthew 22:37
Jesus said unto him, Thou shalt love the Lord thy God with all thy heart, and with all thy soul, and with all thy mind.

Unfortunately, I believe that 'True Bible Salvation' is fast becoming a thing of the past. It has become an unbiblical….feel good…. just as you are…..stay as you are…no repentance type of salvation message today. God is love… yes He is…..but God is also just and righteous. There is very little preaching on sin. We like to tip toe around sin and by doing so we fail to show how our sin breaks the Law of God and how this has placed us in a very dangerous position……… separated from God and on our way to eternity separated from God.

Preachers no longer get their messages on their knees, seldom getting the Holy Spirit engaged in the preparation and presentation of their preaching. Good old fashioned Bible oriented Gospel Hymns and Doctrinal type preaching and teaching on sin and Biblical principals have been replaced by chanting choruses, rock music, and messages that have nothing to do with where we are in our daily struggle to maintain a Christian walk with the Lord. Christians today have lost that deep personal connection with the Bible and the God of the Bible. In fact, many Christians today have never experienced a deep personal relationship with the Lord. There is a disconnect today between Mom and the Lord or between Dad and the Lord or between Mom and Dad and the Lord, the Church, the Preacher, the Christian School and our children have seen it and have been caught up in it and they just wanted out. And that is why it is the Grandparents who are now taking the Grandchildren to Church, while our 'Born Again' sons and daughters are sitting at home. *(Praise the Lord for Godly Grandparents)*

I have had many conversations with parents whose sons or daughters no longer come to church. Many parents cling to the old but favoured explanation that their children made a profession of faith in Sunday school or Junior church and regardless of how they are currently living their adult lives, they are sure that they are saved.

Here is a thought for you; maybe some of our children, who made a profession of faith when they were young, were never really saved in the first place. Maybe some of our own children will someday stand before the Lord and have a *Matthew 7: 21-23* experience.

Matthew 7: 22 – 23
21. Not every one that saith unto me, Lord, Lord, shall enter into the kingdom of heaven; but he that doeth the will of my Father which is in heaven.
22. Many will say to me in that day, Lord, Lord, have we not prophesied in thy name? and in thy name have cast out devils? and in thy name done many wonderful works?

23. And then will I profess unto them, I never knew you: depart from me, ye that work iniquity.

What a horrific experience this will be for some of the people we love the most. This should be a very sobering thought for many of us who have children sitting at home with absolutely no interest in the Lord and no desire to be around Christians. Many Christians misquote *Proverbs 22:6*. This verse is not saying that if our children go off into sin, they will come back to the Lord when they get older. Rather, I believe it is teaching us that if we train up our children properly in their youth, they will continue in their walk with the Lord and will not depart as they grow into adulthood.

Proverbs 22:6
Train up a child in the way he should go: and when he is old, he will not depart from it.

If our children have no desire to be around Christians..... if they have no desire to read their Bible....if they have no desire to pray.....if they have no desire to go to church.....if they have no desire to take their own children to church.....if they have no desire to follow the Lord and have no appetite for the things of the Lord.....then quit kidding yourself about the profession of faith they made when they were young.

John 10:27
My sheep hear my voice, and I know them, and they follow me:

Matthew 7:20
Wherefore by their fruits ye shall know them.

Maybe... *just maybe...* your son or your daughter is one of those who made a profession of 'Faith' when they were young children or maybe even as a young adolescent or teen. Maybe they are in fact saved and are just in a backslidden condition. But are you willing to take that chance? I am not saying that young children cannot get saved; of course they can and they do! I am just saying that when it comes to the most precious possessions we have; our own children; we should become fruit inspectors. And if our children show absolutely no sign of spiritual life then we need to become fervent prayer warriors on their behalf. If one of our children suddenly fell to the floor and stopped breathing we would rush to their side and immediately begin mouth to mouth and call 911. The Church has to wake up and realize that one of the greatest battles today is the battle for the hearts, minds and souls of our children and Satan is winning. Instead of trying to entertain our young people with a razzle dazzle jazzed up music program, and allowing them to play games in the teen room during the Sunday morning service, we need to get them back into the Sunday morning service to hear the preaching and teaching of salvation by grace through faith and get them to the point of true repentance and turning from sin. They need to know that there are consequences for their sin and that there is a price to pay if they neglect salvation and reject the price that has already been paid. If we could get a vision of one of our own children (or a loved one) entering eternity separated from God and dropping off into Hell it should drive us to our knees in prayer.

However, in many situations it will take more than just prayer to turn some of our young people and loved ones around.

Mark 9:29
And he said unto them, This kind can come forth by nothing, but by prayer and fasting.

Fasting is a lost discipline in Christian circles today. We no longer know the purpose for, nor do we know the principles of Fasting.

Ephesians 6:12
For we wrestle not against flesh and blood, but against principalities, against powers, against the rulers of the darkness of this world, against spiritual wickedness in high *places*.

We all face spiritual battles today that at times completely overwhelm us. These battles should make it clear how much we are in need of prayer and fasting. Our Soul is made up of our mind, our emotions and our will and Prayer and Fasting helps to bring all three of these aspects back into line with the mind of Christ and into subjection of the will of God for our lives. We need the Spiritual wisdom and direction for our lives, our homes, our children and our grandchildren, that can only come to us through the Word, through prayer and through fasting.

Fasting is not an option. The Lord has made it clear in His Word that He expects us to fast..........

Matthew 6:16 Moreover when ye fast ....
Matthew 6:17 But thou, when thou fastest, anoint thine head, and wash thy face....

It will become very clear that if you compared the Authorized King James Bible with the modern day Bibles on the scriptures concerning fasting, the KJV Bible stands alone in making this principle very clear. Compare Matthew 17: 19–21 in the KJV with many of the modern bibles (NIV, ESV, NASB, NKJB etc.) and you will find that they have either cut out vs. 21 …..*Howbeit this kind goeth not out but by prayer and fasting*…or they have a foot note stating that this verse is not found in the Greek Text that they have used. (more on the comparisons of scripture later)

Fasting is a part of our Christian heritage and involves so much more than just missing a meal or going hungry.

Isaiah 58:6
Is not this the fast that I have chosen? to loose the bands of wickedness, to undo the heavy burdens, and to let the oppressed go free, and that ye break every yoke?

When we consider some of our children and our grandchildren, we as parents and grandparents have a great need to pray and fast in order to loosen the bands of wickedness, to undo the heavy burdens and to set them (and us) free from oppression and to break every yoke..........*Fasting and Prayer* is the key and we need to get back to it!

"*One Book Stands Alone*" by Dr. Douglas Stauffer has a phenomenal chapter on Fasting. I highly recommend this book if you are serious about learning and understanding the Biblical principle of fasting.

This brings me to the very point of why I am writing another book on the Bible?

I have spoken with parents who are heartbroken over children who enjoyed going to Sunday School and AWANA and yet no longer have any interest in going to church. I believe the problem starts at the *'Foundation of our Faith'* and this is where I may differ with many people today. Many feel that in order for us to keep our young people in church we need to get with the times. Many believe that we need a more upbeat music program (Christian rock) and that we need more preaching on the love of Jesus with less emphasis on sin and repentance.

Many people today believe that our young people need to be entertained, where I believe they need to be trained.

Many of our young people have no spiritual depth and are therefore very vulnerable to the pressures put on them by the world and by the Prince of Darkness himself. They have no *Spiritual Foundation*.

Just what do I mean when I say 'Foundation of our Faith'?

I believe that the *Foundation* for the *Authority* of our lives should be the Word of God and here in lies the problem. For years new Bibles have poured into the market on a regular basis. Many of these Bibles stand in stark contrast to the Authorized King James Bible. The target market for these 'New Bibles' are Christians and many have bought into the program.

For several hundred years the King James Bible was the Foundation upon which our Protestant Church was anchored. Today however, we question its authority and no longer hold to it as the inspired, infallible and perfect Word of God. There are no longer any absolutes; now we are enlightened; now we are into something 'New' and 'Up-to-date' and 'Different'. The liberal ecumenical Evangelicals are winning and solid Conservative Fundamentalism is hard to find.

It is not difficult for me to understand how a High School science teacher in one semester...just one semester...can unravel our children's faith and undo years of Church, Sunday School, Awana, Youth Groups etc.

When was the last time you ever heard a message on the Bible? Some Preachers have never studied how we got our Bible. They just don't know. They simply go with the flow and do not want to ruffle any feathers. However, some came out of Seminaries or Bible Colleges that have thrown out the Greek New Testament of the Received Text / Textus Receptus and had professors who taught from the Nestle's Greek Text (UBS) which is the 1889 revision of the Greek New Testament of Westcott & Hort. These are the Preachers who cut their teeth on the King James Bible as a young person in their home Church and because of some misguided professor they are now using the NASB, NIV, ESV, the 'New' King James or the 'New Scofield Reference... or some other New Revision or New Translation.

Let me stop for a minute to say this; I know that there will be many who will disagree with almost everything that I am about to share in this book, however, my concern is with our young people. They need to see and hear the other side of the equation concerning the Word of God. I do not know of any church that is teaching the Doctrine of Divine Inspiration together with the Doctrine of Divine Preservation. Our young people need to hear these Biblical truths so that they can come to their own conclusion on whether the Word of God is in fact the Word of God... is it Inspired...is it inerrant... can it be trusted... who is God and what are His expectations for their lives?

I believe that most of the men who no longer read or teach from the Authorized King James Bible are good Godly men who love the Lord, and many are a much better Christian than I am. I want to emphasize once again that the purpose of this book is not to attack their character nor their personal spiritual walk with the Lord. Many of them are very sincere, dedicated men who have definitely been called by the Lord into the ministry and have left home and country to serve the Lord and to teach and preach the Word of God. As a Christian, I have to respect that and I do. However, even though I believe they are very sincere in what they are doing, I also believe that they are sincerely wrong if they have laid aside their King James Bible for one of these modern day bibles.

Sadly, some of today's Preachers who are currently preaching from the Authorized KJV teach that the KJV is their Bible of choice, but then go on to teach that it contains errors and that only the 'Original Texts' were Inspired. This line of reasoning escapes me. I do not know how a person can preach and teach from a Bible that they believe to have errors in it? Where would they draw the line? What verse, what chapter has errors in it? How would they have the confidence to know whether the verse they are preaching or teaching is Truth or Error? More importantly, what kind of a message does this send to our young people, our teens, the new Christians or even the mature Christian members of the Church? This kind of teaching leads to confusion and confusion leads to apathy.

Romans 10:17
So then faith *cometh* by hearing, and hearing by the word of God.

Our 'Faith' is supposed to be predicated on the Word of God. With a new Bible and/or a revision of a new Bible hitting the market on a yearly basis, everything concerning the Word of God is in constant change. The foundation upon which the early Church was built is being destroyed and this is why I felt the need to write this book.

Psalms 119:172
My tongue shall speak of thy word: for all thy commandments *are* righteousness.

I am not a scholar. I attended the State University of NY at Buffalo on a hockey scholarship and graduated in 1972 with a BS in Education. I was more of a jock than a scholar. I was named in the 'Outstanding College Athletes of America' in 1972 and was inducted into the UB Sports Hall of Fame in 1983. I have never been to seminary nor to a Christian University. I have taken a Home Bible Institute course from a well-known Baptist College. However, this once vibrant soul winning Baptist Church just had a Mormon give the Commencement Address at their University Graduation a couple of years ago and now openly attacks the Authorized King James Bible in their theology classes! How confusing is that for the young people there?

Let me give you some things to think about.

Today we sit in our beautiful homes, food on the table, and a roof over our heads and we are indifferent and unaware of the people who were hunted down; burned at the stake; tortured; beheaded and terrorized over the writing of the Bible into the English language. We take so much for granted.

What do you know about the Bible you read i.e. your Bible of choice? Do you know which 'Texts' were used to translate your Bible of choice into the English language? Do you know the history of the English Bible that you are currently using? Who wrote your Bible of choice? When and where was it written? Do you understand and believe in the Doctrine of Divine Inspiration? Do you understand and believe in the Doctrine of Divine Preservation?

In what language were the 'Original Texts' written? Where are these 'Original Texts' today? If you do believe in the Doctrine of Divine Inspiration, then you have to understand and come to the conclusion that there was a time when, and a place where, God inspired one true set of Old Testament Scriptures from Genesis to Malachi and one true set of New Testament Scriptures from Matthew to the Revelation of Jesus Christ. The battle that we face today is not so much about the Doctrine of Divine Inspiration. Most Christians will agree and confirm that they believe in some form of Divine Inspiration. The argument that many Christians have today is over the issue of Divine Preservation. If the Lord through Divine Inspiration has promised to Preserve His Word, then which one of the Bibles that we have available for us today is in fact a copy of the True, Inspired, Inerrant and ***Preserved*** Word of God?

John 12:46–50
46. I am come a light into the world, that whosoever believeth on me should not abide in darkness.

47. And if any man hear my words, and believe not, I judge him not: for I came not to judge the world, but to save the world.
48. He that rejecteth me, and receiveth not my words, hath one that judgeth him: the word that I have spoken, the same shall judge him in the last day.
49. For I have not spoken of myself; but the Father which sent me, he gave me a commandment, what I should say, and what I should speak.
50. And I know that his commandment is life everlasting: whatsoever I speak therefore, even as the Father said unto me, so I speak.

John 12: 46-50, is a powerful piece of Scripture that deals with the Word of God.

You need to look at vs. 49 and meditate on it. Give it some very careful and mindful consideration. Go over it several times and let it sink into your heart of hearts. Someday people will stand before God and be judged by the Living Word of God, however, this judgment would be without merit, if God was not able to provide a copy of the Inspired Word of God for people to read down through the ages.

What is the Final Authority upon which we are to build our lives? Is it not the Holy Bible? Has the Lord provided a 'Copy' of the 'True, Inerrant, and Inspired Word of God' for us today? And if He did; then Which One is it? There can only be one!

God only wrote one Bible.

This book is based on the 'Presupposition' that the Bible is the Verbal, Plenary, Inspired Inerrant Word of God and is therefore without Error and Perfect.

Chapter Three

INSPIRATION / PRESERVATION / LITERAL INTERPRETATION

There is a war raging for the hearts and minds of Christians and yet many Christians are completely unaware of this war. It is a war that started at the very Beginning of Time; back in the Book of Genesis and will not end until there is 'time no longer'. *(Revelation 10: 5 -6)*

Lucifer is the vile and wicked Anointed Cherub, who many believe was with the Trinity when they spoke the Universe into existence. This same vile and wicked Angel is still very active today in what he does best; attacking the Word of God and causing doubt and confusion amongst God's People.

Genesis 3:1
Now the serpent was more subtil than any beast of the field which the LORD God had made. And he said unto the woman, Yea, hath God said ....

This wicked fallen Angel that rebelled against God has not changed his position nor his desire to become God. He is still as vile and subtle as he was in *Genesis 3:1* and has continued to attack the Word of God down through the ages.

Isaiah 14:12–15

12. How art thou fallen from heaven, O Lucifer, son of the morning! *how* art thou cut down to the ground, which didst weaken the nations!
13. For thou hast said in thine heart, I will ascend into heaven, I will exalt my throne above the stars of God: I will sit also upon the mount of the congregation, in the sides of the north:
14. I will ascend above the heights of the clouds; I will be like the most High.
15. Yet thou shalt be brought down to hell, to the sides of the pit.

What is the Foundation for Our Authority as Christians?

There is only 'One Foundation' upon which we as Christians should recognize as our 'Authority'. It is not the Church. It is not 'fallible' man and /or the words of 'fallible' man. It is not a hierarchy of religious fallible men of which Christ spoke against in *Revelations 2:6*. It is not any one group of leaders, whether Catholic, Protestant or Jewish.

A Sovereign God has chosen to reveal Himself through 'The Word of God'...'The Holy Bible'. All that we currently need to know about God on this side of Heaven is contained in the Bible. All that we need to know about the nature and condition of man is also contained in the Bible. God the Father through Divine Inspiration of the Holy Spirit has revealed Himself through His Son, Jesus Christ, who is the express image of the Father and is The Living Word of God. The Foundation for our Authority as Christians is 'The Word of God'.

Hebrews 1:1–3

1. God, who at sundry times and in divers manners spake in time past unto the fathers by the prophets,
2. Hath in these last days spoken unto us by *his* Son, whom he hath appointed heir of all things, by whom also he made the worlds;

3. Who being the brightness of *his* glory, and the express image of his person, and upholding all things by the word of his power, when he had by himself purged our sins, sat down on the right hand of the Majesty on high;

The Doctrine of Divine Inspiration

When I speak of the Doctrine of Inspiration, I understand it to be the verbal, plenary and Divine Inspiration of God's Word. Next to Jesus, the Holy Bible is the most important and precious possession that God has handed down to man. Every word of Scripture was given to man by God and every part of the Bible is of Divine Origin.

The battle today is between two trains of thought:
1. Inspiration and Providential Preservation
2. Limited Inspiration i.e. only the 'Original Documents' were inspired and were not preserved

If you believe that inspiration is limited to the Original Manuscripts then you also believe these Original Manuscripts, which we no longer have at our disposal, have been corrupted over time at the hands of fallible man. However, if you believe that God has providentially protected these inspired Original Manuscripts down through the ages of time, then you believe that the Bible is in fact the verbal (the words), plenary (all parts equally) and Divine Word of God.

Inspiration was the direct act of God the Holy Spirit whereby He 'breathed out' the very words of God to ***specially prepared men of God*** (using their individual personalities, their language and their writing styles) to produce the Old and New Testaments in the original languages. (Hebrew, Aramaic and Greek)

As surely as God breathed the breath of life into the nostrils of Adam and man became a living soul, so God breathed

Inspiration / Preservation / Literal Interpretation

into the mind and heart of these ***prepared men of God,*** the exact words that He wanted them to write.

The Bible is a God breathed Book. The Bible is an Inspired Book. It is without error and it is perfect.

2 Peter 1:20–21
20. Knowing this first, that no prophecy of the scripture is of any private interpretation.
21. For the prophecy came not in old time by the will of man: but holy men of God spake *as they were* moved by the Holy Ghost.

The word 'moved' in the Greek means carried along like a Sail Boat with the wind in the sails moving the boat along. The boat in and of itself possesses no power to move itself across the water. The movement of the boat relies totally on the wind. The Bible was not written by the will of man. Man possessed no wisdom, nor power in or of himself, to write Scripture. No prophecy of the Scripture is of any private interpretation. Our Bible was delivered to man by the very breath of God and carries with it the absolute divine authority of an Omnipotent Creator God. The Bible is a book in which we can place our complete and total faith and trust.

2 Timothy 3:15–17
15. And that from a child thou hast known the holy scriptures, which are able to make thee wise unto salvation through faith which is in Christ Jesus.
16. All scripture *is* given by inspiration of God, and *is* profitable for doctrine, for reproof, for correction, for instruction in righteousness:
17. That the man of God may be perfect, throughly furnished unto all good works.

Did Timothy have at his disposal the Original manuscripts of the Book of Genesis that were written by the hand of Moses or the Psalms that were penned by the very hand of David or was Timothy reading from the 'Preserved Copies' of the inspired Old Testament scriptures?

I submit to you that these were the Copies of the inerrant and perfect Word of God that still serve as our foundation for doctrine, for reproof, for correction and for our instruction in righteousness today.

The Bible is an Inspired Book........David thought so
2 Samuel 23: 1–2

1. Now these *be* the last words of David. David the son of Jesse said, and the man *who was* raised up on high, the anointed of the God of Jacob, and the sweet psalmist of Israel, said,
2. The Spirit of the LORD spake by me, and his word *was* in my tongue.

The Bible is an Inspired Book.........Paul thought so
1Thessalonians 2:13

For this cause also thank we God without ceasing, because, when ye received the word of God which ye heard of us, ye received *it* not *as* the word of men, but as it is in truth, the word of God, which effectually worketh also in you that believe.

The Bible is an Inspired Book.........Peter thought so
2Peter 3:15–16

15. And account *that* the longsuffering of our Lord *is* salvation; even as our beloved brother Paul also according to the wisdom given unto him hath written unto you;
16. As also in all *his* epistles, speaking in them of these things; in which are some things hard to be understood, which they that are unlearned and unstable wrest, as *they do* also the other scriptures, unto their own destruction.

The Bible is an Inspired Book.........Jesus thought so
Mark 12: 35–36

35. And Jesus answered and said, while he taught in the temple, How say the scribes that Christ is the Son of David?
36. For David himself said by the Holy Ghost, The LORD said to my Lord, Sit thou on my right hand, till I make thine enemies thy footstool.

Matthew 4:4
But he answered and said, It is written, Man shall not live by bread alone, but by every word that proceedeth out of the mouth of God. (*Deuteronomy 8:3*)

Luke 1: 68–70
68. Blessed *be* the Lord God of Israel; for he hath visited and redeemed his people,
69. And hath raised up an horn of salvation for us in the house of his servant David;
70. As he spake by the mouth of his holy prophets, which have been since the world began:

    Many of today's scholars and so called intellectuals make the mistake of saying such things as "the Book of Hebrews was written by Paul because of this phrase, or because of that word...etc." However, the Book to the Hebrews was handed down to man (Paul) through the operation of the Holy Spirit i.e. Divine Inspiration. God having prepared Paul used his personality, his vocabulary and writing style to give us the original Book of Hebrews in the Greek language.
    The Book of Hebrews is the inspired, inerrant and perfect Word of God which was written and settled in heaven before the foundation of the world and the creation of man.

Psalms 119:89
For ever, O LORD, thy word is settled in heaven.

Matthew 13:34-35
34. All these things spake Jesus unto the multitude in parables; and without a parable spake he not unto them:
35. That it might be fulfilled which was spoken by the prophet, saying, I will open my mouth in parables; I will utter things which have been kept secret from the foundation of the world.

The Inspiration of Scripture cannot be Limited to the Originals.

Divine Inspiration must be extended to the copies of the Originals as well. Timothy was obviously reading from the copies of the Old Testament Hebrew manuscripts (*2Timothy3:15-17*) and these were referred to as 'holy scriptures'.

When the Apostle John penned the last words in the Book of the Revelation; "The grace of our Lord Jesus Christ *be* with you all. Amen"; the *'process of inspiration'* was over, the canon was closed and the Bible was complete. There are no revised editions of any of the Books in the Bible that are currently hiding in a cave waiting to be discovered and added to the canon of Scripture. The *'process of inspiration'* is over, however, the *'product of inspiration'* is still going on today.

The *'product of inspiration'* is when one takes the Masoretic Texts of the Hebrew Bible which are an exact copy of the Original Hebrew manuscripts and *translates* these Hebrew Words into another language, with words that express the exact same meaning as the Hebrew words in the Original texts, then that translation is a copy of the inspired and inerrant Word of God. The same can be said about the Textus Receptus. If one takes the Textus Receptus which is an exact copy of the original Byzantine Greek manuscripts and *translates* these Greek words into another language with words that express the exact same meaning as the Greek words in the Original, then that *translation* is also considered to be the inspired and inerrant Word of God as well.

Isaiah 46: 9–10

9. Remember the former things of old: for I *am* God, and *there is* none else; *I am* God, and *there is* none like me,
10. Declaring the end from the beginning, and from ancient times *the things* that are not *yet* done, saying, My counsel shall stand, and I will do all my pleasure:

    The Bible contains sixty-six different books, the result of the inspired writings of some 40 different men of God spanning over 1500 years, in three different languages (Hebrew, Aramaic & Greek) and on three different continents. Most of these men lived in different centuries and different countries. They were unaware of each other and each other's prophecies and some even quoted from books not yet written. Only God could do that! Many lived miserable lives and died horrible deaths. In spite of all this, the Bible from Genesis to the Revelation is a flawless perfect record of everything we need to know about God. It contains historical, poetic, geographic and doctrinal themes that were supernaturally handed down to man through the operation of God the Holy Spirit. One would think that with so many writers, spread out over 1500 years, on three different continents that there would be a vast number of contradictions and discrepancies, however, the Bible has proven to be totally consistent from beginning to end. To the world it must appear that there was some kind of collusion among the writers to produce a Book that is so flawless and with a continuity that cannot be explained apart from the hand of God. Down through every generation from the beginning of time, many unbelievers have made it their mission to destroy the Scriptures. None have prevailed. God the Holy Spirit breathed the very words of God into the heart and mind of man and has providentially guarded and protected these inspired documents down through the ages. That is why we call it the 'HOLY BIBLE'.

The revelations of God's Truth are something that did not come from the imagination of man nor are they something that man could know apart from God. The words contained in the Bible are as a whole and in every part God's Word to us.

The first five books of the Old Testament, the Pentateuch, were written by Moses in the Hebrew language because that was the language he spoke. However, we need to understand that it was not the language that was inspired but rather the message, the revelations of God in the Hebrew language that were inspired. God in His foreknowledge knew that Hebrew would be the language of His chosen people, and He therefore inspired the Old Testament in the Hebrew language (some Aramaic) and has providentially kept and protected it down through the ages.

The very existence of a Jewish state called Israel is one of the greatest miracles of modern day history. This nation was destroyed and dispersed to the far ends of the earth for centuries. In 1948 the Nation of Israel was re-gathered to their ancient homeland and re-established once again. Even nations who can trace their existence back to antiquity cannot match the miracle of Israel. In the days of the Pharaohs, Egypt wasn't Arab, but Coptic. Ancient Babylon wasn't Arab, but Chaldean. Today we have a modern Israel that has retained ancient bloodlines, religious customs, traditions and their ancient language is intact. The working language of modern day Jerusalem is the same Hebrew spoken in King David's time. Israel's Jewish nature is as unique today as it was a thousand years before Mohammed. The circumstances surrounding the existence of the Nation of Israel are utterly unprecedented and only God could do that.

When the Holy Spirit spoke to the heart of Moses, he not only received these God given revelations about creation, Adam and Eve, the Patriarchs, the Law, etc., he then put them to print in the Hebrew language. Therefore every word and all parts equally as written by the very hand of Moses are the inspired Word of God in the Hebrew language.

The same can be said of the New Testament. God in His providence had the New Testament written in the Greek language as that was the language of the day. The Original manuscripts of the New Testament were copied and sent to the early Apostolic Churches where they were cherished and jealously protected by the Holy Spirit.

In order for us to fulfill the Great Commission, God knew it would be necessary to have His Word translated accurately, word for word, in the languages of the world. The translation of the Bible into any language is of the utmost importance to those by whom the language is spoken. Translating the Bible into the English language was by far the most important event that ever took place in the history of modern man. The Authorized King James Bible has been read by millions of people for centuries and still remains a translation that is considered by many today to be a work of the highest order.

In *Matthew 4:4* Jesus tells us that we are to live by every word that comes out of the mouth of God and then in *Matthew 5: 17-18* Jesus makes an emphatic statement about these words.

Matthew 5: 17–18
17. Think not that I am come to destroy the law, or the prophets: I am not come to destroy, but to fulfil.
18. For verily I say unto you, Till heaven and earth pass, one jot or one tittle shall in no wise pass from the law, till all be fulfilled.

The 1828 Webster Dictionary:
Definition of the word jot – an iota; a point; a tittle; the least quantity assignable

Definition of the word tittle – a small particle; a minute part; a jot; an iota

Jesus it telling us in *Matthew 5:17-18* that He did not come to destroy the law as contained in the first five books of the Old Testament Scriptures (Moses) nor did He come to destroy the Scriptures of the Prophets (Isaiah, Ezekiel, Daniel etc.) but rather He came to fulfill all that was written in both the law and the prophets concerning Him.

Not only was He coming to fulfill these Scriptures in general terms, He was coming to fulfill every single point right down to the smallest minute part or jot or tittle of these Scriptures.

Psalm 119:160
Thy word *is* true *from* the beginning: and every one of thy righteous judgments *endureth* for ever.

Who then is man to detract in even the smallest degree from the inerrant, infallible, and inspired Words of a Sovereign God? We do so at our own peril. *(Revelations 22: 18–19)*

The Doctrine of Divine Preservation
We need to look at the twin sister of Inspiration i.e. the Doctrine of Divine Preservation. God not only inspired His Pure Words; God also promised to **'Keep'** and **'Preserve'** them.

Psalm 12:6–7
6. The words of the LORD *are* pure words: *as* silver tried in a furnace of earth, purified seven times.
7. Thou shalt keep them, O LORD, thou shalt preserve them from this generation for ever.

Psalm 119:89
For ever, O LORD, thy word is settled in heaven.

Psalm 119:152
Concerning thy testimonies, I have known of old that thou hast founded them for ever.

1 Peter 1:23-25
23. Being born again, not of corruptible seed, but of incorruptible, by the word of God, which liveth and abideth for ever.
24. For all flesh *is* as grass, and all the glory of man as the flower of grass. The grass withereth, and the flower thereof falleth away:
25. But the word of the Lord endureth for ever. And this is the word which by the gospel is preached unto you.

One of the most convincing of all proofs and arguments for Inspiration and Preservation, is when Jesus himself regards and treats them as such.

Luke 24:44-45
44. And he said unto them, These *are* the words which I spake unto you, while I was yet with you, that all things must be fulfilled, which were written in the law of Moses, and *in* the prophets, and *in* the psalms, concerning me.
45. Then opened he their understanding, that they might understand the scriptures,

What scriptures in *Luke 24* did Jesus open their minds to understand? Did they have the Originals or did they have Copies of the Originals? Did they have the hand written Original Manuscripts from Moses or did they have a 'Copy' of the Books of Genesis, Exodus, Leviticus, Numbers and Deuteronomy in the Hebrew language that God in His providence had preserved for them to read? I submit to you that the hand written Originals of the Old Testament were long gone during the days and ministry of Jesus.

Most Christians will agree that God inspired His Word in the Originals. But what about God's promise to keep and preserve His Word ......"from this generation for ever"? How many Christians believe this to be true?

What happened on the day of Pentecost?
The Inspired and Preserved Word of God went out with equal authority and clarity in all the languages represented by all the nations in Jerusalem on that day.

Acts 2:8 And how hear we every man in our own tongue, wherein we were born?

Romans 16:25–26
25. Now to him that is of power to stablish you according to my gospel, and the preaching of Jesus Christ, according to the revelation of the mystery, which was kept secret since the world began,
26. But now is made manifest, and by the scriptures of the prophets, according to the commandment of the everlasting God, made known to all nations for the obedience of faith:

The Holy Spirit inspired Paul to write and make it very clear what God's mindset was concerning the preaching of the Word and the circulation of the Scriptures; to make the Word of God known to... all nations... for the obedience of faith... and that my friend is the Great Commission! Not only are we to preach the Gospel concerning Jesus but we are to take this Gospel to all the nations of the world.

Would a person have to be fluent in Hebrew/Aramaic and Greek to read and understand the Inspired Word of God or to teach or preach the Word of God?

If a translation into another language uses the preserved copies of the original Hebrew Old Testament Scriptures and the preserved copies of the original Greek New Testament in a word for word translation and thus provides an exact and accurate translation of the true, inerrant and infallible Word of God, then it is a copy of the Inspired Word of God in that language. In like manner, if one then takes a Translation that was predicated on this premise e.g. the Authorized King James Bible and uses this Translation to translate the Bible into German or Spanish or French etc. with words that are accurate and express the exact same meaning as the English words then they have a copy of the Inspired Word of God as well.

The belief in Divine Inspiration and Divine Preservation is what sets (or should set) Christians apart from the Humanistic Textual Criticism of Unbelievers today. Believers must operate from the *'Presupposition'* that the Word of God came through the Operation of God the Holy Spirit and that God has *'Preserved'* His Inspired Word. The Holy Spirit breathed the very words of God into the hearts of men. These holy men of God not only spake as they were moved by the Holy Ghost; they also put the words of God to the written page and God has *'Providentially'* cared for and *'Protected and Preserved'* His Word down through every dispensation of time and in the many languages of the known world.

Taking the Word of God to the World is our mission and it should be our passion!

<u>Literal Interpretation of the Bible</u>

When we think of the Doctrine of Inspiration together with the Doctrine of Preservation and realize that we have a copy of the perfect Word of God at our disposal, then how are we as Christians supposed to interpret the Word of God? The answer to this question is found in the Word of God itself.

2 Timothy 3:16
16. All scripture *is* given by inspiration of God, and *is* profitable for doctrine, for reproof, for correction, for instruction in righteousness:

Matthew 4:4
But he answered and said, It is written, Man shall not live by bread alone, but by every word that proceedeth out of the mouth of God. (*Deuteronomy 8:3*)

Some people believe that the literal interpretation of scripture means that we are to take every letter and every word, regardless of the context or form of expression and interpret the verse exactly the way it is expressed. ***For example:*** **Psalm 91:4** *He shall cover thee with His feathers and under His wings shalt thou trust…..*therefore God is a bird with wings and feathers.

One may laugh at that inference but that is how some people judge a *'Literalist'*. However, this is what is referred to as *'Letterism'* and there is a very marked and distinct difference between *'Literalism'* and *'Letterism'*.

The *'Literalist'* would say the following about *Psalm 91:4*. "This is obviously an allegory which gives us a picture of God overshadowing and protecting His children as a hen does her chicks." That is how a *'Literalist'* would interpret this passage and this would be consistent with other scripture and consistent with the context of the verse and content of the Bible when talking about the nurturing and loving character of our God.

A *'Literalist'* is someone who believes that the Bible is the inspired and inerrant Word of God and therefore takes God at His Word, because God's Word is perfect.

Since the Lord is the originator of "All" and every language and desires to communicate His word to every man in every corner of the world, then it would stand to reason that He would communicate from His heart to the heart of man

Inspiration / Preservation / Literal Interpretation

in a language that would be concise and clear and written in such a way that we could understand it in a literal, normal and plain sense.

When I hold my Authorized King James Bible in my hand, I am confident that I have an exact copy of the inspired and preserved Word of God in the English language. Not only is the King James Bible an exact copy of the Inspired Word of God, it is written in a format that is concise, clear and easy to understand.

This is the purpose of the Bible...God communicating from His heart to the heart of man.

Matthew 15:10
And he called the multitude, and said unto them, Hear, and understand:

I am certain that the Lord wants us to hear the Word of God and to understand what He is saying. Why would I not take the inerrant and clear word of God literally? Often we hear someone say, "God said it.....I believe it.....that settles it." However the truth is; God said it.....and whether you believe it or not.....it is already settled.

A Pure, Perfect, Immutable God handed down His Pure, Perfect and Immutable Word to holy men of God. These holy men of God then put these Words of God to pen and paper, so that you and I would have an exact 'Copy' of the very Words of God available to us today.

I cannot remember where I got the following article on *Malachi 3:3*, however, it is a perfect story on the Pure Word of God. *(Psalms 12: 6–7)*

Malachi 3:3 And he shall sit *as* a refiner and purifier of silver:

Malachi 3:3 puzzled some women in a Bible study and they wondered what this statement meant about the character and nature of God. One of the women offered to find out the process of refining silver and get back to the group at their next Bible study. That week, the woman called a silversmith and made an appointment to watch him at work. She didn't mention anything about the reason for her interest beyond her curiosity about the process of refining silver. As she watched the silversmith, he held a piece of silver over the fire and let it heat up. He explained that in refining silver, one needed to hold the silver in the middle of the fire where the flames were hottest to burn away all the impurities. The woman thought about God holding us in such a hot spot; then she thought again about the verse that says: "And he shall sit *as* a refiner and purifier of silver:" She asked the silversmith if it was true that he had to sit there in front of the fire the whole time the silver was being refined. The man answered that yes, he not only had to sit there holding the silver, but he had to keep his eyes on the silver the entire time it was in the fire. If the silver was left a moment too long in the flames, it would be destroyed. The woman was silent for a moment. Then she asked the silversmith, "How do you know when the silver is fully refined?" He smiled at her and answered, "Oh, that's easy; when I see my image in it".

And that is exactly what the Word of God is; the very image of the Master. It has been purified in the fire seven times: it is 'Pure' 'Inerrant' 'God Breathed' and 'Perfect'. You can see the face of God in its pages and God won't be satisfied until He sees His image in you.

Psalm 12:6
The words of the LORD *are* pure words: *as* silver tried in a furnace of earth, purified seven times.

Whenever we are going through the fire, remember we are in the hands of the Master Silversmith and He is in the process of conforming us to the image of His Son.

Romans 8:29
For whom he did foreknow, he also did predestinate *to be* conformed to the image of his Son, that he might be the firstborn among many brethren.

I use the word *'literal'* in its dictionary sense i.e. what does the word mean as it is presented in the dictionary ....the natural or usual meaning of the word....the ordinary and apparent sense of the word...of a writing....or of an expression....and NOT some allegorical or metaphorical meaning.

When it comes to studying the Word of God, I have several very important tools at my disposal. The first is a 'Strong's Concordance' which is the most complete and widely accepted concordance of the King James Bible. Every word in the Bible is listed with every passage where the word is found. The Concordance contains a brief dictionary of both the Hebrew and Greek words as they are found in the original with references to the English words that apply. The second tool is the '1828 Noah Webster American Dictionary of the English Language'. This dictionary takes one back in time and proves to be an invaluable tool for looking up a word from the KJV to see not only what the meaning of the word is but also how it may have been applied or used back in the days of the Translators.

There is another phenomenal tool that I cannot get along without. It is a free download called e-Sword. (Free is a good Baptist word) If you do not have a Strong's Concordance it is available on e-Sword and much easier to access than the book itself. It also provides many other translations of the various English Bibles which allows me to do a parallel comparison of scripture verses and words. I also have two commentaries available through e-sword; Barnes' Notes and Mathew Henry's. If you do not have 'e-sword' then download it from the internet. It is one of my favourite tools for Bible study and did I mention that it is free!

I was once in a situation when a dear friend who reads and studies from the Authorized King James Bible, took a very strong position that even though the KJV is his Bible of choice, we have to understand that there are errors in it. He is of the opinion that only the Originals are inspired. He then used *Genesis 22:1* as the sample verse to prove his point and compared it to *James 1:13*.

Genesis 22:1
And it came to pass after these things, that God did tempt Abraham, and said unto him, Abraham: and he said, Behold, *here* I *am*.

James 1:13
Let no man say when he is tempted, I am tempted of God: for God cannot be tempted with evil, neither tempteth he any man:

The word *'tempt'* in *Genesis 22:1* in my friends mind was an *'error'* in the KJV Bible. He based this position on the comparison with *James 1:13*.

However, the same Hebrew word translated 'tempt' in *Genesis 22:1* was also translated 'tempt" in *Deuteronomy 6:16*.

Deuteronomy 6:16
Ye shall not tempt the LORD your God, as ye tempted *him* in Massah.

The Same Hebrew word is used for both passages – with a different meaning in each case.

<u>Strong's Concordance:</u>
Genesis 22:1 tempt H5254 the Hebrew word ***Nas-sah***
Deuteronomy 6:16 tempt H5254 the Hebrew word ***Nas-sah***

Nas-sah is a primitive root; to test, by implication to attempt, adventure, assay, prove, tempt, try

The 1828 Webster Dictionary: *Gives two basic definitions for the word 'tempt'*
1. One is to evil
2. One is to testing or proving

The 1828 Webster Dictionary's definition of 'tempt' lines up with Strong's Concordance.

Barnes' Notes on the Bible gives a very good interpretation of *Genesis 22:1*
Genesis 22………Verses 1-19

"God tests Abraham's unreserved obedience to his will. "The God." The true, eternal, and only God, not any tempter to evil, such as the serpent or his own thoughts. "Tempted Abraham." To tempt is originally to try, to prove, put to the test. It belongs to the dignity of a moral being to be put to a moral probation. Such assaying of the will and conscience is worthy both of God the assayer, and of man the assayed."

Assay; means to try or prove by experiment, the quality and purity of metallic substances, so when Barnes uses the word "assay" , he is saying that God was testing the quality and purity of Abraham's will and conscience in obeying His Word. God was not 'Tempting' Abraham as in the context of *James 1:13*.

James 1:13-14
13. Let no man say when he is tempted, I am tempted of God: for God cannot be tempted with evil, neither tempteth he any man:
14. But every man is tempted, when he is drawn away of his own lust, and enticed.

Strong's Concordance: James 1: 13–14
Tempted G3985 Peirazo
From G3984 to test (objectively) that is endeavour, scrutinize, entice, discipline: assay, examine, go about, prove, tempt (-er), try
This is the same meaning for the Hebrew word H5254 *Nas-sah*

Barnes' Notes: James1:13
"Neither tempteth he any man. That is, he places nothing before any human being with a view to induce him to do wrong. This is one of the most positive and unambiguous of all the declarations in the Bible, and one of the most important. God does not place inducements before us with a view that we should sin, or in order to lead us into sin. None of his decrees, or his arrangements, or his desires, are based on that, but all have some other purpose and end. The real force of temptation is to be traced to some other source; to ourselves, and not to God."

When we teach from *Genesis 22:1*, we can with confidence state that the word 'tempt' in this verse of scripture means to test or to prove. Temp is an accepted English word that means not only tempted to evil, but rather in this situation and in the context of this passage and consistent to the teaching of the Bible, the word tempt here in *Genesis 22:1* means to test or to prove. God was testing Abraham's unreserved obedience to His will. So the word 'tempt' as found in *Genesis 22:1* is not an 'error' in the KJV Bible.

Another example of this can be found in Luke 14:26
Luke 14:26
If any *man* come to me, and hate not his father, and mother, and wife, and children, and brethren, and sisters, yea, and his own life also, he cannot be my disciple.

Inspiration / Preservation / Literal Interpretation

Some cults teach that children are to hate their parents and family and come live in some commune completely devoted to the Spiritual leader and drink the cool aid with no questions asked. This of course, would be taking the verse way out of context and would be inconsistent with the overall teaching of family relationships in the Bible. The Bible is clear that our relationships with our families are to be loving, caring and respectful towards one another. (*Ephesians 5: 21-25 and Ephesians 6: 1-4*)

Luke 14:26 deals with our attitude towards Christian service and the cost and the price that some will pay when picking up their cross and following Him.

We therefore, have to be very careful in our interpretation of Scripture because it is of no private interpretation. The Bible should only be understood via the normal use of language i.e. with the use of normal words; in the light of historical and cultural backgrounds, and in the context of the passage, and consistent with the overall teaching of the Bible i.e. one word or one passage or one text does not contradict the other when we look at the entire package. The Bible is God's Book and there are no contradictions or errors in it.

When someone starts to say that there is a problem with the Word of God, then all sorts of red flags should be going up and alarms going off.

How does one rightly divide the Word of Truth if you do not believe that it is in fact the Word of Truth and that it can be trusted for what it is clearly saying i.e. as it is written and within the context in which it appears? God has placed His Book in our hands. It has the image of His Face in its pages; read it; trust it; obey it. It will serve you well.

This is an old cliché:

"If the plain sense makes good sense; seek no other sense; lest it results in nonsense."

Dr. David Cooper the founder of The Biblical Research Society put it this way.....

"When the plain sense of Scripture makes common sense, seek no other sense. Therefore, take every word at its primary ordinary, usual, literal meaning. Unless the facts of the immediate context, studied in the light of related passages and axiomatic (self-evident) and fundamental truths indicate clearly otherwise"

Why is it that some people refuse to take God at His word and refuse to believe that God would give man an Inspired Book that would tell us exactly who He is and that this Book would be written in such a way and in a language that we can clearly understand? So clear in fact that even a Child can hear it and understand it. In every case that I know of, the opponents of the *'literal interpretation'* of the Scriptures have to, (by necessity) reject the above position because they have to make the Bible fit into their *'Theological Positions'*.

It should therefore come as no surprise that large portions of God's word often get metaphoric and/or allegoric interpretations. Things like the literal six days of creation in Genesis; a literal Adam and Eve; the rebuilding of the temple in the last days as given in vivid detail in Ezekiel 40 through 48 and confirmed in Revelation; Daniel's 70 weeks; the 1000 yr. Kingdom in Revelation; the 3 ½ yrs. found in Daniel and Revelation; the animal sacrifices and the Millennial Temple and many other portions of scripture have to be changed or interpreted outside of the natural and simple sense of their meaning and context. Why? Because to interpret the Bible in a simple and literal way does not fit into their theology. They believe that God didn't really mean it when He made a covenant with the Nation of Israel and that Isaiah was talking about the Church and not Israel.

One of the first King James Bibles that I read was the Thompson Chain Reference Bible. In the book of Isaiah it made reference on the top of the pages to "the Church comforted" and "restoration of the Church" etc. However, the Book of Isaiah has nothing to do with the Church and everything to do with the Nation of Israel. Many theologians today believe and teach that God's covenant to David, the Davidic Covenant, now belongs to the Church.

Someday soon we will see the truth of the Word of God unfold before our very eyes as God fulfills His covenant and His promises. The World will soon discover that the Nation of Israel, is still the apple of His eye.

Deuteronomy 7:9
Know therefore that the LORD thy God, he *is* God, the faithful God, which keepeth covenant and mercy with them that love him and keep his commandments to a thousand generations;

Zechariah 2:8
For thus saith the LORD of hosts; After the glory hath he sent me unto the nations which spoiled you: for he that toucheth you toucheth the apple of his eye.

When push comes to pull and you are confronted with those who do not believe in God or His Book then just ...... let God be true, but every man a liar......(*Romans 3:4*)

Psalm 118:8
It is better to trust in the LORD than to put confidence in man.

Proverbs 22:19–21
19. That thy trust may be in the LORD, I have made known to thee this day, even to thee.
20. Have not I written to thee excellent things in counsels and knowledge,
21. That I might make thee know the certainty of the words of truth; that thou mightest answer the words of truth to them that send unto thee?

I believe the Bible says what it means and means what it says. It is a God breathed book that is perfect and without error. The literal interpretation of scripture is simply taking God at His Word….add nothing to it….and take nothing away from it.

If I could give a word of advice and leave you with one thought, it would be this: make sure you do in fact have a copy of the true and inspired Word of God and then just………..

"Take God at His Word"

Chapter Four

TEXTUAL CRITICISM OF THE BIBLE

There are Basically only Two Streams of Bibles
Genesis 3:15
And I will put enmity between thee and the woman, and between thy seed and her seed: it shall bruise thy head, and thou shalt bruise his heel.

Here in *Genesis 3:15* we see the beginning of the battle between Satan and the coming Christ Child. Satan immediately went to work to try to destroy the blood lines; Cain murdering his brother Abel was just the start of his attack and if you read *Genesis 6: 1–8,* you will see and understand how wicked the world had become under the direct interference of Satan; so much so that God had to bring the Flood to put an end to it.

This attack by Satan continued down through the ages to the days of King Herod in *Matthew 2:16*, where Herod went out and had all the children from 2 years old and under killed in an attempt to kill the King of the Jews; the Christ Child. Satan must have thought that he had finally succeeded in killing the Christ Child on the Cross at Calvary but how disappointed he must have been when death was swallowed up in Victory and 'Up from the Grave He Arose with a mighty Triumph ore his foes!'

1 Corinthians 15: 54–57
54. ......Death is swallowed up in victory.
55. O death, where *is* thy sting? O grave, where *is* thy victory?
56. The sting of death *is* sin; and the strength of sin *is* the law.
57. But thanks *be* to God, which giveth us the victory through our Lord Jesus Christ.

After years of attacking and failing to destroy the person of Jesus Christ, Satan set his mind to work on something just as evil. Satan set out to corrupt and change God's Inspired Word and to center his attack on destroying the Church from within.

Why do you think we have so many different Bibles available today? A generation ago if someone asked which Bible is the true Bible, the only answer you would have received is the Authorized King James Bible. Today, however, there is an uncertain sound coming from many pulpits and class rooms. Confusion amongst Christians over the Word of God has become widespread and sometimes contentious. How often have you been sitting in a Sunday School class where everyone is taking a turn to read a verse in a certain chapter, and someone reads a verse that is completely different and may even have a slightly different meaning and everyone, looks up with that...'What was that'... look on their face?' Could this be the reason why most churches today no longer have the congregation stand together for the reading of God's Word before the Preaching?

The First Stream of Bibles

The Old Testament for this First Stream of Bibles is based on the Ben Chayyim Masoretic Text which was the Text for the Hebrew Bible that was found in the early Apostolic

Churches. These early Apostolic Churches also had a New Testament based on the Text of the Byzantine Greek New Testament or the Textus Receptus. These precious Bibles were providentially preserved and protected in Churches such as the Church at Pella in Palestine where Christians fled from the destruction of Jerusalem by the Romans in 70 A.D, by the Syrian Church of Antioch, by the Italic Church in northern Italy, by the Gallic Church of southern France, by the Celtic Churches in Great Britain, Scotland and Ireland and by the Waldensian Church and the churches of the Reformation.

There is a vast volume of literature on these churches to substantiate the fact that there is very little difference between all of these Protestant Bibles that used these Greek and Hebrew Manuscripts to translate the Bible into their various and many languages. They all had as their foundation the copies of the 'Original, Plenary, Inspired, Inerrant Word of God that were providentially protected and preserved as promised in *Psalm 12: 6–7*.

From this stream of Bibles came our English King James Bible of 1611.

The Second Stream of Bibles

The second stream of Bibles is a small one and based on very few manuscripts.

The New Testament was based on the Greek Texts of the Alexandrian Manuscripts of the Vaticanus Codex B and the Sinaiticus Codex Aleph. In rejecting the Textus Receptus, Westcott and Hort put together a new 'Greek New Testament' that was based on these Greek texts. (***Today it has been revised to the Nestle-Aland &/or the UBS Greek Texts with both maintaining the same foundation i.e. the Alexandrian manuscripts***)

They also had the Latin Vulgate which was changed (corrupted) into the Latin Bible of Jerome. In English they have the Jesuit Bible of 1582, which went through some vast changes in the Douay Rheims or Catholic Bible.

For the Old Testament they went with the Ben Asher Text (Leningrad Manuscripts 1008AD) which many theologians believe to come from a handful of corrupt manuscripts that contain approximately 30,000 changes to the trusted Ben Chayyim Masoretic Text.

This second stream of Bibles formed the foundation for the 1881 Revised Bible of Westcott and Hort. They completed their New Testament in 1881, the Old Testament in 1885 and the Apocrypha in 1894.

The Revise Bible of 1881 gave birth to the American Standard Version in 1901 and to most if not all of the modern day Bibles that are flooding our Churches today.

Take your Bible of choice and check the preface. If you read from a modern Bible you will probably find a reference to the Septuagint, LXX for short. The translators used the Septuagint along with the other texts to translate your Bible. (NKJV included) They claim that the Septuagint contains true readings not found in the preserved Hebrew Masoretic text, however, the Septuagint is one of the most corrupt documents that the Catholic Church has ever perpetrated on the Church. The Septuagint considers the Apocrypha to be divine scripture and have mixed these in with the books of the Bible. At best the Septuagint is a hoax and should never be accepted as the authoritative Word of God.

Many Preachers today believe in 'limited' Inspiration and therefore believe and teach that all the Bibles available today, including the KJV, have errors. In their effort to avoid **confrontation,** many preachers have allowed **confusion** to enter into the Church and we know that God is not the author of confusion.

1Co 14: 32–33
32. And the spirits of the prophets are subject to the prophets.

33. For God is not *the author* of confusion, but of peace, as in all churches of the saints.

If God is not the author of confusion, then who is?
In light of these two streams of Bibles, we need to look into the subject of **Textual Criticism**. Once we do this we will be able to understand the mindset and thought process of the Translators of the two streams of Bibles that we have today.

Biblical Textual Criticism:

We need to take a look at **Biblical Textual Criticism** and how it played a major part in the Modern Day Bibles that have flooded into the Church. Old Books of Antiquity are filled with ancient knowledge and culture. The originals of many of the most ancient books are no longer with us. We know about these ancient documents because of the copies. Someone made a copy of the Original Manuscript or Document or Text and then another copy of the copy was made. We have to remember we are talking about documents that were hand written and came to us over very long periods of time. Over the centuries some of the words of the original manuscript or document or text were lost or deliberately left out from one copy to another. Textual Criticism can therefore be described as the study of these ancient documents. It is an attempt to estimate the damage to the Text or a Manuscript or a Document and then to repair or restore it back to its *Original Condition*.

Let me give you an example: Josephus (37AD – 100AD)
Also known by his Hebrew name, Yosef ben Matityahu; Joseph the son of Matthias. Josephus was a Renowned 1st Century Jewish historian who was fluent in Aramaic and Hebrew. His writings provide an important historical and cultural insight into the days of Jesus and the New Testament era. He wrote on the lives of James the Just who he called the Brother of Jesus. He also wrote about John the Baptist,

the High Priest Annas and Pontius Pilate. He is most noted for his writings on Jesus called the Messiah. You have to understand that the 'Original Documents' of Josephus are long gone. Therefore the 'Textual Critics' must look at the 'ancient copies' of the Manuscripts of Josephus and decide if they are genuine; are they the real deal; are they authentic? This debate has been going on since the 17th Century. That is what Textural Critics do. They piece together pieces of ancient documents and try to make it whole, or as close to the Original as possible. They try to authenticate Texts and piece them together.

Is the Bible just Another Book from Antiquity?

Is the Bible just another one of man's books from Antiquity? Has the Text of the Bible been damaged over time and do we therefore apply the same Textual Criticism to the Bible that we apply to other Ancient Books of Antiquity; like the writings of Josephus; or books like the Iliad; or Greek Mythology?

Today all of the 'Original' hand written manuscripts or texts of the Bible are gone. Nobody in today's world has seen or handled the Original Book of Genesis; it is gone! Today we have the Copies of the Copies of the Copies etc.

In a leading Baptist Church and University, the Preacher who built his ministry on the foundation of the King James Bible, took a very strong stand against the King James Only Movement. In the process he openly attacked good Christians who were not a part of this King James Only Movement but who believed in both the Doctrine of Divine Inspiration and Divine Preservation of their King James Bible. This Preacher made some very disparaging remarks and leveled accusations of heresy towards Christians who held the position that the King James Bible was the Inspired and Preserved Word of God. One of his Theology Professors in the University said this concerning *I John 5:7- 8*. "Thus, according to John's account here, 'there are three that bear record in heaven'. The rest of verse 7 and the first nine words of verse 8 are *not in the original manuscripts* and are not to be considered as part of the Word of God." Obviously, both the Preacher and his Professor of Theology believed in 'Limited Inspiration' and therefore 'Limited Error' of Scripture and therefore do not believe in the Doctrine of Divine Preservation. To them this position would be considered heresy.

How does this Professor know these words are not in the Original? How does he know? Does he have the Original hand written Greek Manuscript that the Apostle John wrote? If this Baptist University professor were honest, he should have said that these words in *1 John 5:7- 8* are not in *some* of the manuscripts that are considered by *some* intellectuals to be the most ancient. Actually, this Baptist Professor should have said that they are not found in the Greek Manuscripts of the Vaticanus Codex B or the Sinaiticus Codex Aleph from the *Second Stream of Bibles.* However, if he were to be totally honest he would have said that they are in fact found word for word in many of the Greek New Testament manuscripts that scholars agree and believe to be extant from the Byzantine Text, (Textus Receptus) that served as the foundation for the New Testament in *the First Stream of Bibles.*

The Old Latin translations of the New Testament are very important in establishing the authenticity of *I John 5:7-8*. Latin was the major language up through the Middle Ages. The Old Latin is not the same as the Latin of Jerome's Vulgate, which by the way, does include *1 John 5:7-8*. The Old Latin predates the Vulgate text and is found well into the Middle Ages.

The Tepl Codex, a fourteenth century manuscript written in Middle High German which came from an Old Latin manuscript (w) from the 15th century is significant because it actually predates the Vaticanus and Sinaiticus documents and contains the verse that has been rejected by so many liberal minded Theologians today. The Tepl Codex contains this verse exactly as it is found in the *Textus Receptus*. Imagine that!

The Waldensian Church has been dated back to about A.D. 120, which puts them back into the days when some of the Apostles were alive and still ministering. History teaches that they lived in the Vaudois valleys in France until they were savagely persecuted by the Church at Rome and were driven high into the Alps of northern Italy between the fourth and thirteenth centuries. Their Old Itala Bible was translated in the early second century and is therefore a document that predates the Tepl Codex of the fourteenth century. Research into the text and history of the Waldensian Bible has shown that it is a literal descendant of the Old Itala. In other words, the Itala has come down to us in Waldensian form, and firmly supports the Traditional Text, the Textus Receptus. The Waldensian Bible is a translation of the true text into the rather rude Low Latin of the second century and this Bible of the Waldensians was used to carry this true text throughout Europe.

The translators of the AV 1611 King James Bible did not simply include this verse because it was in Erasmus' edition of the Greek New Testament, they had four Bibles on their tables that had come under heavy Waldensian influence. All four contained *1John5:7-8* just as it was contained in the ***Textus Receptus***. The first of these was the Geneva Bible which was translated in 1557 at Geneva, the center of the Swiss Reformation. The basis for the Geneva Bible was the French Olivetan which was translated by Olivetan, a Waldensian pastor and relative of John Calvin. This fact illustrates how readily the two streams of descent of the Textus Receptus through the Greek East and the Waldensian West, ran together and provides a wonderful example of the *Providential Hand of God* in the *Preservation of His Word*. In addition to these four Bibles, there is reason to believe that the King James translators had access to at least six Waldensian

Bibles written in the old Waldensian vernacular, all of which contained the disputed passage.

Most modern translations are based upon the Alexandrian text-type tradition (i.e. Sinaiticus and Vaticanus). When you compare these versions with the Authorized KJV you will clearly see, that there is a substantial omission and consequent mix-up of the text. The modern versions completely remove verse 7, as found in the King James Bible; then the phrase "in the earth" is taken out. Then the first phrase of verse 8 (There are three that bear witness) becomes verse 7. Thus, the entire arrangement and sense of the passage is altered i.e. they have taken away from and added to the Word of God.

Unfortunately, this altering of the text is often accepted without question. In fact, the issue is rarely, if ever, reasoned through in modern times. Accusations against the passage's authenticity are simply announced as though they were facts. (Liberals are experts at this kind of posturing) These liberal minded professors conclude that there is no evidence that can be mounted in favor of the authenticity of *1 John 5: 7-8*. This, however, is far from the truth.

So when this Baptist professor or any professor or preacher or teacher takes this kind of position on the Word of God then we know the foundation upon which they have built their Biblical mindset.

1 John 5: 7-8 (KJV)
7. For there are three that bear record in heaven, the Father, the Word, and the Holy Ghost: and these three are one.
8. And there are three that bear witness in earth, the Spirit, and the water, and the blood: and these three agree in one.

1 John 5: 7-8 (Modern Bible)
7. For there are three that testify
8. The Spirit, the water and the blood; and the three are in agreement.

Do you see the subtle attack on the 'Trinity' in *I John 5: 7-8* in the Modern Translation?

The omission of 'the Father, the Word, and the Holy Ghost in vs.7 and 'these three agree in one' in vs. 7 & 8 is a direct attack on the Trinity. What kind of effect would this have on a young teenage student who is sitting there with his or her Authorized King James Bible and is subjected to this kind of teaching in their Theology class?

Jesse M. Boyd from Wake Forest North Carolina has written a phenomenal Exegesis called 'And These Three are One', it is an absolute must read concerning this portion of scripture and can be found on line. This is the other side of the coin. You owe it to yourself to read this article and 'Study to shew thyself approved unto God, a workman that needeth not to be ashamed, rightly dividing the word of truth.' (*2Timothy 2:15*)

Note: *Jesse M Boyd attended the same Baptist University in question above concerning the passage in 1John5:7-8. The arguments that Jesse M Boyd put forth were never challenged by the faculty of the University on a substantive basis, instead they simply dismissed his Exegesis and attacked his character. He was a brilliant student who received a BA in Religion with a minor in Greek all with a straight 'A' 4.0 grade. i.e. until his Exegesis for which he received an 'F'. Attacking someone's character is what Liberals do best when they have no substantive argument. How sad is that?*

I used to read from the Scofield Reference Bible. It is still in my library and I still refer to it from time to time. One needs to be careful when studying from a reference Bible and/or a Concordance. The men who put these reference Bibles and Concordances together often come out of Seminaries that do not hold to the Masoretic Hebrew texts for their Old Testament nor the Textus Receptus for their Greek Bible and therefore their marginal notes and references may not hold true to the Word of God.

If you have a Scofield Reference Bible turn to *1 John 5:7* and you will notice a little "o" in front of verse 7. Now look in the center reference section and you will find the "o" where Mr. Scofield says, *"It is generally agreed that v. 7 has no real authority, and has been inserted."*

I'd like to ask Mr. Scofield where, when and how he came into contact with the 'Original' hand written manuscript of the Apostle John? Mr. Scofield had never seen it; had never handled it; had never read it; because it was no longer available. The Original is gone. Some religious intellectual at the seminary he attended probably taught him this lie. It was probably the same intellectual who taught Mr. Scofield about the Gap Theory.

If Satan cannot get someone to actually change the text of the Word of God, he then lurks in the marginal notes causing confusion and doubt. Satan never stops his vile, methodical and subtle attack on the Word of God.

By the way, *the 'New King James Version'* has the same type of foot note in the margin for *1John 5:7* as well. Go figure? Listen, can you hear the *hissssss*..…yea hath God said?

Many believe and teach that the NKJV is just a modern revision of the hard to understand English of the Authorized King James Bible. It is not. (more on the NKJV later)

In light of what the Bible says in *Revelation 22:18–19*, I think that one should be very careful when making these kind of statements concerning the Word of God.

Revelation 22: 18–19

18. For I testify unto every man that heareth the words of the prophecy of this book, If any man shall add unto these things, God shall add unto him the plagues that are written in this book

19. And if any man shall take away from the words of the book of this prophecy, God shall take away his part out of the book of life, and out of the holy city, and *from* the things which are written in this book.

It is not difficult for me to understand why this once leading Baptist College has taken the name Baptist out of its name when it achieved University status and has since had a Mormon deliver the Commencement Speech to a recent Graduation Class. I guess they must believe that the Mormon Jesus is the same as our Biblical Jesus. Now who is bordering on heresy? Is not the Mormon Church considered a cult? Hmmmm......... yea hath God said? It has become clear to me that this once great Conservative Christian Church and College has become part of the ever growing all-inclusive liberal Evangelical ecumenical movement. I believe the Bible is crystal clear concerning a Mormon addressing a Christian University graduation class.

By the way, the Mormon that spoke at this University is a wonderful individual that I listen to almost every day on his radio program. I am bit of a political junkie and find him to be a straight shooter. I appreciate the fact that there are no gray areas in his stand on the political issues of the day. So this is not an attack on his person nor his character. He is an amazing family man who takes an uncompromising stand on supporting the Constitution of the USA. He is a dedicated and open Mormon who loves and supports the nation of Israel and lives a very principled disciplined life style. I just find it hard to understand how a Christian University, whose Doctrinal Statement speaks of a Trinity of God the Father, God the Son and God the Holy Spirit, could justify having a Mormon address the students at their Commencement when their Trinity is made up of Joseph Smith, Elohim and Jesus? That would be like having Jack Hyles address the graduating class at Brigham Young University and expecting the Mormon leadership and the members of the faculty to be ok with it. Jack Hyles was a great preacher who would have certainly been up for the challenge, however, what we have here are two very different Biblical Positions on Salvation and far too many other doctrines that run contrary to one another.

This would be like trying to mix Oil and Water; not going to happen. I believe this Christian University sent the wrong message to their staff, to their students as well as to other likeminded Christian Universities and Colleges.... but this kind of behaviour has become the new norm and is just a sign of the times and the beginning of things to come!

Galatians 1:8–10
8. But though we, or an angel from heaven, preach any other gospel unto you than that which we have preached unto you, let him be accursed.
9. As we said before, so say I now again, If any *man* preach any other gospel unto you than that ye have received, let him be accursed.
10. For do I now persuade men, or God? or do I seek to please men? for if I yet pleased men, I should not be the servant of Christ.

In the realm of New Testament Textual Criticism, the *Mindset* or the *Presuppositions* of the Modern Day Textural Critic are completely hostile to our historic Christian Faith. Before they even start to examine the thousands of documents and manuscripts from which our Bible was translated into the English language they have already presupposed or predetermined in their minds that the Bible or Scripture was written by man and not by God. To the carnal unsaved mind of the Natural Textual Critic, the Bible is just another book that was written by fallible man and therefore subject to error and corruption over time.

1 Corinthians 2:14
But the natural man receiveth not the things of the Spirit of God: for they are foolishness unto him: neither can he know *them*, because they are spiritually discerned.

The modern day unsaved liberal Textual Critics want to *destroy* the Bible. Most of them are highly educated secular humanists who do not believe in God and have no desire to follow any of the moral principles as found in the Word of God. They do not believe in the verbal inspiration nor the preservation of God's Word. They want to destroy the Bible believing Church and everything that we hold near and dear to us as Bible believing Christians. Every generation has had a vast army of these non-believers who have made it their life work to disprove and destroy the authenticity and authority of the Scriptures. They want to take the Bible out of our Schools, out of our Government and out of our Homes. Their desire is to destroy everything that is Christian.

That is their Mission... That is their Goal...
That is their Passion.

So what Must we do as Christians?
Our Scriptures admonish the Christian to walk by faith and not by sight.

2 Corinthians 5:7
7. (For we walk by faith, not by sight:)

Romans 1:17
17. For therein is the righteousness of God revealed from faith to faith: as it is written, The just shall live by faith.
(Habakkuk.2:4, Galatians.2:20 & 3:11, Hebrews 10:38)

We are instructed by the Word of God to live our lives based on 'Faith'. And we are told that our 'Faith' is anchored to the Word of God. The Word of God is critical and essential in order for us to determine exactly what 'Faith' is. (more on this later)

Romans 10:17
17. So then faith *cometh* by hearing, and hearing by the word of God.

We as Christians must not build our Textual investigation of Scripture based on the foundation of the carnal presuppositions of the modern day Secular Humanist. We must by 'Faith' build our investigation *of the Bible... on the Bible... The Word of God.*

Our Textual Investigation must begin with and be built upon the Inspired Word of God.

1 Corinthians 2:12 – 13
12. Now we have received, not the spirit of the world, but the spirit which is of God; that we might know the things that are freely given to us of God.
13. Which things also we speak, not in the words which man's wisdom teacheth, but which the Holy Ghost teacheth; comparing spiritual things with spiritual.

Our Investigation Must start with the following Presuppositions:
1. The Bible is not just another one of the many Books of Antiquity
2. The Bible is Inspired and contains the very Words of God
3. The Bible is the Providentially Preserved Word of God
4. Our Faith; Our Beliefs must rest on the Solid Rock of Holy Scripture

As Christians we Must base our Biblical Textual Criticism on:
1. The Doctrine of Divine Inspiration of the Bible
2. The Doctrine of Divine Preservation of Holy Scripture

You cannot separate these two Doctrines and according to *1Corinthians2:13*, we must "compare spiritual things with spiritual".

If the Bible is not inspired then there is no need for preservation and if God was unable to Preserve His Word for us today, then Inspiration holds no value or worth. All that would remain would be some secular humanistic philosophical book authored by fallible man and the world and the Church today is flooded with this kind of dribble.

It is important for Christians to investigate the Biblical Textual Criticism that has given the English Bible to the World. We need to investigate how the Doctrine of Inspiration and Preservation played out in the minds of the Translators of the English Bibles that are currently in the World today. Who were the Textual Critics and which 'Documents or Manuscripts' did they use to give you the Bible of your choice?

Isaiah 46:9
Remember the former things of old: for I *am* God, and *there is* none else; *I am* God, and *there is* none like me,

Isaiah 46:10
Declaring the end from the beginning, and from ancient times *the things* that are not *yet* done, saying, My counsel shall stand, and I will do all my pleasure:

Malachi 3:6
For I am the LORD, I change not..........

Chapter Five

THE AUTHORIZED 1611 KING JAMES BIBLE

Is it possible for a Christian to know which Bible is in fact the express Word of God?

It is my desire that your faith in the Word of God will be rekindled in your heart of hearts and that you will cultivate a new and deeper relationship with the author and finisher of your faith the Lord Jesus Christ, the living eternal Word of God.

Over the centuries Satan has tried to destroy the Bible. 'Foxes Book of Martyrs' is a powerful story about the Christian men, women and children who were hunted down, tortured, and burned at the stake for possessing a copy of the Word of God in the English language. Christians had to hide their English Bibles and meet together in secrecy. When we gather at the Bema Judgement Seat of Christ, how many of us would count ourselves worthy to stand beside these Christian heroes of the faith and watch them get their rewards.

Today we have Christians in Communist &/or Muslim countries who are very familiar with this kind of persecution. A Bible is the most treasured and cherished possession that these underground Christians and Churches have. We who live in North America, can go to Church and openly carry our Bibles without any fear of persecution, however, in far too many homes, our Bibles sit on a book shelf and we treat them as *'just another book'*.

I highly recommend a message from Dr. Kirk DiVietro; "Who Suffered for Bible Preservation". Please go on line and listen to this message. I guarantee it will rip your heart out.

Let's take a look at the First Stream of English Bibles.

The first stream of Bibles have an Old Testament based on the Masoretic Hebrew Texts and a New Testament based on the Manuscripts of the Textus Receptus of the early Apostolic Church. These serve as the foundation for our Authorized King James Bible of 1611.

Hebrews 10:38
Now the just shall live by faith....

2 Corinthians 5:7
(For we walk by faith, not by sight:)
As Christians.........We are to walk by *'Faith'* not by *'Sight'*

Romans 10:17
So then faith *cometh* by hearing, and hearing by the word of God.

According to the Word of God the Christian is to live by faith. God in His Wisdom gave man His Word; The Bible. The Bible is how God communicates with man today. That is how He speaks to our hearts and minds. God no longer speaks directly through His audible voice from a 'burning bush' or from a 'cloud' or from a 'mountain top'. We are to get 'Our Faith' from the Word of God and we are to put 'Our Trust' in the Word of God. If we are to live by 'Faith' and if we are to build our lives on the Word of God, then how are we to effectively do this if we no longer have a true and trusted copy of the 'Inspired Word' of God?

Many Christian Universities and Colleges have rejected the Greek New Testament of the early Apostolic Church as the foundation for their theology. They have been taken in by the intellectual ramblings of men like Tragelles, Tischendorf, Westcott and Hort etc. They want us to believe that the Lord gave us the Inspired Word of God once; way back in the days of Moses and way back in the days of David and way back in the days of the Apostles; but today we have manuscripts that have been corrupted over time at the hands of fallible man.

Are we to neglect the teaching of ***Psalm 12:6-7*** and believe that God was unable to protect and preserve His Word for us today? Are we to believe that a Sovereign, Omnipotent, Omniscient, Omnipresent God, who spoke a universe into being, did not have the power or the ability to keep and preserve His Inspired Words for us today as He promised? Let's see if this line of reasoning holds water with what we believe.

We, who believe in the Divine Inspiration of Scripture believe in a Creator God....

1. Who literally spoke a universe into existence from nothing; just spoke and it was there!
2. Who then set His universe into motion; all the galaxies, planets, stars, moons; all moving in uniform perfection; balanced and in complete harmony; billions of systems within systems and galaxies within galaxies all working together like a Swiss watch.
3. Who designed planet Earth as the centre or highlight of His Creation with a perfect atmosphere, temperature and conditions to sustain all life as we know it.
4. Who went on to create, to fashion, to design every kind of living plant, tree, flower, insect, fish, animal, bird, mammal, everything from mammoths to microscopic cells invisible to the human eye; with each life form intricately interwoven and working together in perfect harmony and balance; a flourishing Garden of Eden

teaming with millions upon millions of different kinds of life forms.
5. Who then decided to Create Man; after His Image and after His likeness; and breathed into man the breath of life; and man became a living soul.
6. Who did all this in 6 literal 24 hr. days! And said it was All Good! Can you imagine that!?
7. Who continues to hold everything in His creation together both visible and invisible by His power and His authority. (Colossians 1: 10–19)
8. Who through an operation of the Holy Spirit gave man an Inspired Book that tells us everything that we need to know about Him from Creation to Salvation.
10. Who not only gave us an Inspired Book but then promised to keep and preserve His Pure Words. (Psalm 12:6-7)
11. A God who not only set His glory above His creation but then elevated His Word to a position above His name.

Psalm 8:1 To the chief Musician upon Gittith, A Psalm of David.
O LORD our Lord, how excellent *is* thy name in all the earth! who hast set thy glory above the heavens.

Psalm 138:2
I will worship toward thy holy temple, and praise thy name for thy loving kindness and for thy truth: for thou hast magnified thy word above all thy name.

And now some unsaved humanistic textual critic or some misguided Preacher or Professor wants me to believe that My God was unable to preserve a copy of His Word for me today... Really? They want me to believe that my God just abandoned His Word; the most precious gift He ever handed down to man (next to Jesus). Am I supposed to believe that my God took His perfect, inerrant, written Word and just threw it out there and allowed time and man to take away from it, add to it and thus corrupt it... Really? Is that the God you believe in?

The Word of God is absolutely essential for our Salvation and for our ability to live a victorious Christian life. The Word of God, the Bible, is to be the Final Authority and the Foundation for our lives. Do you believe for one minute that our Lord would abandon such an important document? Do you believe that our Lord would not protect a Book that He personally handed down to man through the operation of the Holy Spirit? A Book that we need so that we might know Him and understand His wonderful plan of salvation? Do you really believe that a Sovereign Creator God did not have the presence, the power, the wisdom or the wherewithal to providentially take care of His Word over time? A God who knows when a sparrow falls to the ground was unable to keep and protect His Inspired Word.

Matthew 10:29
Are not two sparrows sold for a farthing? and one of them shall not fall on the ground without your Father.

I want to take a moment to share an experience that I had while sitting 20 feet up in my deer stand. It was a beautiful November morning and I was reading my Bible as I patiently waited for a deer to show itself. I just so happened to be reading *Matthew 10:29* and I paused and asked the Lord if He was actually aware of a sparrow when it dies? I mean with everything that is going on in the universe, is it possible for the Lord to be aware of a tiny sparrow as it hits the ground or was this verse just an allegory?

About 20 yards away a bunch of Black Capped Chickadees flew into a tree making all kinds of noise. Suddenly, one of them flew straight at my stand and landed on the very edge of the Scofield Reference Bible that I held in my hands. It stayed there for about 15 to 20 seconds and just looked me up and down. It was like the Lord was saying, "Yes Michael, I really am aware of a sparrow when it falls". Can you imagine the Lord taking the time to show Himself to me in such an amazing way? Hearing the thoughts of my heart and then providing such a graphic answer. I was overcome with a mixture of emotions. I was overjoyed with the up close and personal encounter with that tiny bird and then I was humbled and bowed my head and asked the Lord to forgive me for my unbelief and to thank Him for showing Himself in such a unique and amazing way.

Yes we serve that kind of God; we serve an awesome God; a kind, tender, compassionate God that delights in the fellowship of His children. It was a November morning that I will never forget.

Here is a thought for you to ponder; if Divine Inspiration is an operation of the Holy Spirit (*2Peter 1:20-21*) and our Sovereign Creator God was unable to keep his promise to preserve His Word down through the various dispensations of time, then what about our Salvation? Salvation also involves an operation of the Holy Spirit. He quickens our dead spirit; He indwells us; He seals us; He leads us into all Truth etc. Is our Lord able to protect, preserve and keep our salvation until the day of redemption? Do we have eternal security or can we lose it? Can we believe and trust in the scriptures in *2Timothy 1:12* and *2Timothy 4:18*?

2 Timothy 1:12
12. For the which cause I also suffer these things: nevertheless I am not ashamed: for I know whom I have believed, and am persuaded that he is able to keep that which I have committed unto him against that day.

2 Timothy 4:18
18. And the Lord shall deliver me from every evil work, and will preserve *me* unto his heavenly kingdom: to whom *be* glory for ever and ever. Amen.

Can we trust these verses or are they part of the 'corruption' and 'error' that these so called evangelical, ecumenical textual critics want us to believe have crept into the Bible?

I think that I will stick with the Word of God and just take God at His Word.

James 1: 21–22
21. Wherefore lay apart all filthiness and superfluity of naughtiness, and receive with meekness the engrafted word, which is able to save your souls.
22. But be ye doers of the word, and not hearers only, deceiving your own selves.

John 15:3
Now ye are clean through the word which I have spoken unto you.

It is true that the hand written 'Original Inspired Texts' are no longer available to us today. No one today has seen them and no one today has handled an 'Original' document. The many hand written 'Original' documents from Genesis to Revelation are gone.

In the first twenty years of my salvation I wore out two leather-bound Bibles. Today they sit in my library and if you open them up and turn them upside down the pages will fall out. Can you imagine what happened to the hand written 'Original Text' of the Gospel of John after years and years of people in the early Apostolic Church handling this document and reading from its pages and using it to make copies? How long do you believe this 'Original' document would last?

They did not have the kind of binding or paper and ink that we have today. They had no printing press. Everything was written by hand. This is one of the main reasons why we no longer have the 'Originals' today. The 'Originals' were used and handled so often that they eventually wore out and the worn out 'Originals' were then destroyed once an exact 'Copy of the Original' was finished. What we have today are the 'Providentially Preserved Copies' of the 'Original Texts' as promised by the Word of God in ***Psalm 12:6-7.***

The Bible tells us that our Lord is Immutable: He never changes.

James 1:17
Every good gift and every perfect gift is from above, and cometh down from the Father of lights, with whom is no variableness, neither shadow of turning.

Hebrews 13:8
Jesus Christ the same yesterday, and to day, and for ever.

The Bible also tells us that the Word of God is Immutable as well: It never changes.

Hebrew 6: 13–20
13. For when God made promise to Abraham, because he could swear by no greater, he sware by himself,
14. Saying, Surely blessing I will bless thee, and multiplying I will multiply thee.
15. And so, after he had patiently endured, he obtained the promise.
16. For men verily swear by the greater: and an oath for confirmation *is* to them an end of all strife.

17. Wherein God, willing more abundantly to shew unto the heirs of promise the immutability of his counsel, confirmed *it* by an oath:
18. That by two immutable things, in which *it was* impossible for God to lie, we might have a strong consolation, who have fled for refuge to lay hold upon the hope set before us:
19. Which *hope* we have as an anchor of the soul, both sure and stedfast, and which entereth into that within the veil;
20. Whither the forerunner is for us entered, *even* Jesus, made an high priest for ever after the order of Melchisedec.

Barnes Notes: Hebrews 6: 13–20
"The promises of God are all founded in his eternal counsel and this counsel is an immutable counsel: the promise of blessedness which God has made to believers is not a rash and hasty thing, but is the result of God's eternal purpose; this purpose of God was agreed upon in counsel and settled there between the eternal Father, Son and Spirit. These counsels of God can never be changed; they are immutable and God never needs to change his counsels for nothing new can arise to Him who sees the end from the beginning. The promises of God which are founded upon these immutable counsels of God and confirmed by an oath of God may be safely depended upon, for here we have two immutable things; the counsel and the oath of God, in which it is impossible for God to lie"

God would never do anything that would contradict His nature or His will. The 'immutability of his counsel' is the Word of God. It never changes and God never lies. It is impossible for God to lie. His Word is an anchor to our Soul, both sure and steadfast.

We serve an awesome God!

The Old Testament of our 1611 King James Bible
It must be understood that the Lord committed the writing and keeping of Scripture to the Jews.

Romans 3:1-2
1. What advantage then hath the Jew? or what profit *is there* of circumcision?
2. Much every way: chiefly, because that unto them were committed the oracles of God.

The Old Testament in our King James Bible was translated from the Hebrew Scriptures of the Second Great Rabbinic Bible, or the Ben Chayyim Masoretic Text. The Masoretic Text is named for a group of Hebrew scholars called the Masoretes. They had schools in Babylon and Tiberius by the Sea of Galilee. They flourished from 500 to 1,000 A.D. The word *"Masoretic"* comes from the Hebrew word *'masorah'* which means 'traditional'. The idea is that of both preserving something and passing it down to the next generation. The Masoretes both preserved the Hebrew text and made accurate copies to hand down to succeeding generations. The rigorous care given the Masoretic text in its preparation is credited for the remarkable consistency found in Old Testament Hebrew tests since that time. The Masoretic text enjoyed an absolute monopoly for over 600 years and is universally accepted today as the authentic Hebrew Bible for the Old Testament Scripture. Before Gutenberg invented the printing press in 1452, Scripture had to be copied by hand. The Masoretes were the ones who made these hand written copies. They had to follow certain rules when making a copy of the Synagogue Rolls of the Hebrew Scriptures. These rules are listed in the Talmud and repeated here to show the great care taken in copying the Scriptures.

There were Eight Rules that the Jewish Copyists were Required to Adhere to:

1. The parchment must be made from the skin of a clean animal (clean meaning ceremonially clean according to the Old Testament sanitary laws); must be prepared by a Jew only, and the skins must be fastened together by strings taken from clean animals.
2. Each column must have no less than forty-eight, nor more than sixty lines. The entire copy must be first lined.
3. The ink must be of no other color than black, and it must be prepared according to a special recipe.
4. No word nor letter could be written from memory; the scribe must have an authentic copy before him, and he must read and pronounce aloud each word before writing it.
5. He must reverently wipe his pen each time before writing the word for "God" (Elohim), and he must wash his whole body before writing the name "Jehovah" (LORD in our King James Bibles), lest the Holy Name be contaminated.
6. Strict rules were given concerning forms of the letters, spaces between letters, words and sections, the use of the pen, the color of the parchment, etc.
7. The revision (to correct any errors) of a roll must be made within thirty days after the work was finished; otherwise it was worthless. One mistake on a sheet condemned the entire sheet. If three mistakes were found on any page, the entire manuscript was condemned.
8. Every word and every letter was counted, and if a letter was omitted, or if an extra letter was inserted, or if two letters touched one another, the manuscript was condemned and destroyed at once.

H. S. Miller, writing in his book "General Biblical Introduction", says: "Some of these rules may appear extreme and absurd, yet they show how sacred the Holy Word of the Old Testament was to its custodians, the Jews, and they give us strong encouragement to believe that we have the real Old Testament, the same one that our Lord had and which was given by inspiration of God."

The traditional Hebrew Masoretic Text has been the standard text of the Old Testament for well over two thousand years. It is an explicit example of the Providential Care and Preservation of God's Word and is represented by the vast majority of the existing Old Testament manuscripts. The Masoretes are perhaps the clearest example of true Biblical Textual Critics in action. It does not get any better.

The New Testament of the 1611 King James Bible

The same holds true for the New Testament. The Holy Spirit by divine Inspiration spoke to the hearts of the Apostles (Jews) who then with the same care and dedication of the Old Testament scribes, proceeded to write the New Testament Scriptures in the Greek language. For many years the early Church was privileged to have these hand written Original Manuscripts as penned by Matthew, Mark, Luke, John, Paul, Peter, James and Jude.

History tells us that the Apostle John died in approximately 100AD and many believe that it was John who took on the task of gathering the Greek Texts as written by the Apostles through Divine Inspiration and putting them together in book form that would become the first Greek New Testament for the early Apostolic Church.

Very soon thereafter Satan turned his subtle and evil mind towards the Word of God and the Holy Spirit through the Apostle Paul forewarned the Church over and over about these satanic attacks that were on the way. *2 Thessalonians* is just one example of these warnings.....

2 Thessalonians 2:1–15
1. Now we beseech you, brethren, by the coming of our Lord Jesus Christ, and *by* our gathering together unto him,

2. That ye be not soon shaken in mind, or be troubled, neither by spirit, nor by word, nor by letter as from us, as that is the day of Christ at hand.
3. Let no man deceive you by any means: for *that day shall not come,* except there come a falling away first, and that man of sin be revealed, the son of perdition;
4. Who opposeth and exalteth himself above all that is called God, or that is worshipped; so that he as God sitteth in the temple of God, shewing himself that he is God.
5. Remember ye not, that, when I was yet with you, I told you these things?
6. And now ye know what withholdeth that he might be revealed in his time.
7. For the mystery of iniquity doth already work: only he who now letteth *will let,* until he be taken out of the way.
8. And then shall that Wicked be revealed, whom the Lord shall consume with the spirit of his mouth, and shall destroy with the brightness of his coming:
9. *Even him,* whose coming is after the working of Satan with all power and signs and lying wonders,
10. And with all deceivableness of unrighteousness in them that perish; because they received not the love of the truth, that they might be saved.
11. And for this cause God shall send them strong delusion, that they should believe a lie:
12. That they all might be damned who believed not the truth, but had pleasure in unrighteousness.
13. But we are bound to give thanks alway to God for you, brethren beloved of the Lord, because God hath from the beginning chosen you to salvation through sanctification of the Spirit and belief of the truth:
14. Whereunto he called you by our gospel, to the obtaining of the glory of our Lord Jesus Christ.
15. Therefore, brethren, stand fast, and hold the traditions which ye have been taught, whether by word, or our epistle.

The Old Testament in the Hebrew Language was still very much in use in the Synagogues in the days of the ministry of Jesus. It becomes obvious what Jesus thought of these Old Testament Copies that were in the synagogues during this period. After His temptation in the wilderness Jesus went into the Synagogue on the Sabbath and read from *Isaiah 61: 1-2*.

Luke 4: 15–21
15. And he taught in their synagogues, being glorified of all.
16. And he came to Nazareth, where he had been brought up: and, as his custom was, he went into the synagogue on the sabbath day, and stood up for to read.
17. And there was delivered unto him the book of the prophet Esaias. And when he had opened the book, he found the place where it was written,
18. The Spirit of the Lord *is* upon me, because he hath anointed me to preach the gospel to the poor; he hath sent me to heal the brokenhearted, to preach deliverance to the captives, and recovering of sight to the blind, to set at liberty them that are bruised,
19. To preach the acceptable year of the Lord.
20. And he closed the book, and he gave *it* again to the minister, and sat down. And the eyes of all them that were in the synagogue were fastened on him.
21. And he began to say unto them, This day is this scripture fulfilled in your ears.

Let me say this before we go on with the New Testament. Jesus read from a 'Copy' of the Book of Isaiah. By this time in history the 'Original Text' of Isaiah was gone. Note what Jesus said about this 'Copy' ... "This day is this scripture fulfilled in your ears".

This is a powerful statement concerning the 'Preservation' of God's Word. Jesus considered this 'Copy' to be Scripture, to be the Word of God. He would certainly know this to be true, after all, He is the 'Author' and finisher of our Faith.

When the Apostle John wrote the last sentence in the Book of the Revelation and put down his pen, the Greek New Testament Text was complete and the *process of Inspiration* was closed. This Greek New Testament Text was then committed to the care of the early Apostolic Churches and would become known as **the Byzantine Text; the Textus Receptus; the Received Text or the Traditional Text.**

The greatest enemy of the early Church was not so much the horrific persecution suffered at the hands of the Roman soldiers, but rather the satanic flood of heresy that engulfed the Truth for many years and ushered in the period known as the Dark Ages. During this period of persecution and darkness, the Hebrew Text of the Old Testament and the Received Text of the Greek New Testament were deeply entrenched in these Churches and were jealously protected by God the Holy Spirit as He providentially watched over them. The ***Textus Receptus*** was the foundation for the New Testament Bibles in the various languages as represented in these early churches and it was the Waldensian Church in particular that passed their Bible to the Churches of the Reformation.

It is quite obvious that God wanted His Word translated into all languages. The 'Great Commission' (Mark 16:15) to go into all of the world was followed up by the request in Romans 16:25-26 to take the scriptures into all nations.

Romans16: 25–26
25. Now to him that is of power to stablish you according to my gospel, and the preaching of Jesus Christ, according to the revelation of the mystery, which was kept secret since the world began,
26. But now is made manifest, and by the scriptures of the prophets, according to the commandment of the everlasting God, made known to all nations for the obedience of faith:

As we discussed in Chapter three the Doctrine of Inspiration and Preservation is what sets us apart from unbelieving secular humanism that is so much a part of our world today. We believe that through Inspiration and Preservation nothing was lost as per the translation of the verbal, inerrant, inspired words of the 'Original Texts' into the English language. A careful study of Acts 15 will reveal and confirm the scrupulous care that was exerted by the early Church to guard and protect her sacred writings and with the exception of a few very minor grammatical differences, all of these early New Testament Bibles agreed with one another so closely that many are convinced they were all translated from the same source.

Let's Look at the Traditional Byzantine Text:

There are over 5000 surviving Greek manuscripts available today or as the scholars would say are known to be extant and which contain all or part of the New Testament. The vast majority of these Greek New Testament manuscripts agree with one another so closely (95%) that many believe they all came from the same Greek Text. Most modern day textual critics believe these came from the ***Byzantine Greek Text – the Textus Receptus*** (would also become known as the ***Received Text, the Majority Text or the Traditional Text***) This was the Text that was in use for the greater part of the ***Byzantine Period 312 – 1453.*** This is the Greek New Testament that many believe was gathered and put together by the Apostle John and accepted as Scripture by the early Apostolic Church. This Byzantine Greek New Testament also serves as the Text for the entire ***Greek Catholic Church*** today and is the foundation for the New Testament of our ***Authorized 1611 King James Bible.***

Are we to believe that the Holy Spirit, who Jesus promised would guide us into all truth and bring to remembrance the Word of God, would suddenly abdicate His office, stop His ministry and abandon the Word of God to its own fate? And are we to believe that the New Testament Bible used by the Protestant Church for centuries, was suddenly undone and put on the shelf because of the Alexandrian texts that were lost to the world for over 1500 years? Would God give us a Bible and then hide it in a library at Rome for over 1500 years? Would God give us a Bible that would end up in the garbage in an Alexandrian monastery in Egypt? I don't think so!

The Lord has promised to keep and Preserve His Word and Preserve it He has. It must be remembered that Paul and the other Apostles took many scriptures with them on their missionary journeys. It would be understandable that the Churches at Antioch, Ephesus, Galatia, Corinth, Philippi etc. would make copies of these Scriptures for their own purposes of worship and fellowship.

It was under the authority of the Emperor of Rome, Constantine the Great (306-337) that the ***Textus Receptus*** was rejected and he embraced the heretical writings of Eusebius and Origen that inter-mixed Gnosticism and Christianity. Constantine was responsible for giving the Catholic Church the Eusebio-Origen Bible. However, even Constantine with all his power and authority could not help his 'New' Bible gain acceptance within the Protestant Churches of the Reformation. Despite all of the vicious persecution from the Church at Rome, ***the Textus Receptus*** remained the New Testament Bible of the Protestant Churches for centuries. The Word of God was alive and well and the light of the glorious Gospel pierced through the so called 400 years of darkness and remains with us today. It would do you well to read about the Churches that helped to keep and protect the Word of God, especially the Waldenses from the valleys of the northern Alps of Italy who steadfastly resisted the horrific persecution of the Papacy and passed on to the Reformation a copy of the Word of God which flowed directly from the copies of the Original Greek Text, the ***Textus Receptus***.

Just Another Book

In 1516 Erasmus studied all of the Greek New Testament Texts that were available and restored the **Byzantine Greek Text; the Textus Receptus** to its position of prominence and for the first time in history a printed copy of the Gospel of salvation by 'Grace' through 'Faith' burst into the open for every man to read. For over 400 years (1516–1930) the Greek New Testament of Erasmus (*the Textus Receptus*) would dominate and be used to translate Bible after Bible into the many languages of the known world.

Luther took the Greek New Testament of Erasmus and gave the German people a Bible in the German language. William Tyndale, often referred to as the true hero of the English Reformation, was fluent in 7 languages and was greatly influenced by Martin Luther. He had a great desire to give to the English people what Luther had given to the German people; a Bible that was written so the common man could read and understand God's Inspired Word in the English language. Tyndale was famous for his statement made during a conversation with a high ranking member of the clergy; ***"I defy the Pope, and all his laws, and if God spare my life, ere many years, I will cause a boy that driveth a plough shall know more of the Scripture than thou doest."***

In 1525 William Tyndale took the Greek New Testament of Erasmus and translated the New Testament into the English language. Before Tyndale, the English Bibles were translated from the old Latin Bible. Tyndale was the first one to use the Hebrew Masoretic Bible and the Greek Textus Receptus for his English Translation. It was to become a Bible that the English believers risked life and limb to possess. The Church at Rome was so outraged by the accomplishment of Tyndale, they ushered in a fierce and relentless persecution of anyone caught with any portion of his Bible. The Word of God in the English language was setting the English people free from the tyranny and oppression of the Catholic Church and Tyndale became a man on the run. Eventually in 1536,

Tyndale was caught in the town of Vilvorde in Belgium and was summarily strangled and burned at the stake. He had been feverishly working on the completion of the Old Testament into the English language but was cut short by his unfortunate death. Before the flames licked up around the body of William Tyndale, his last words were a prophetic prayer...*"Lord, open the eyes of the King of England"*.

This prayer would be answered just three years later in *1539*, when King Henry VIII finally allowed, and even funded, the printing of an English Bible known as the "Great Bible" by Miles Coverdale, a prodigy of William Tyndale. He had already completed Tyndale's work with the printing of the entire English Bible in 1535, called the Coverdale Bible. But now he had the full support of the King of England to give the English people 'The Great Bible' and was on the committee for the Geneva Bible of 1560.

However, the true answer to Tyndale's prayer came in *1611*, when King James commissioned a group of Godly men to replace the 1560 Geneva Bible with an updated translation of the English Bible. They used the traditional Ben Chayyim Masoretic Hebrew Text for the translation of the Old Testament and the Textus Receptus for the translation of the New Testament into the English language. Besides the Hebrew Text and the Greek Text, they had the Coverdale Bible, the Bishop Bible, the Great Bible, the Geneva Bible, Tyndale's Bible, as well as all of the known extant manuscripts of the Greek and Hebrew (over 6000) and every foreign version, Latin translations both ancient and recent, the Targums and the Peshitta and all aids as to the elucidation of the Hebrew and Greek Originals. The Lord had 'Providentially' provided everything the Translators would need and use to give us a 'Copy' of the Inspired Word of God in the English language. God had His hand on the writing of the Authorized King James Bible.

Translators of the KJV

The translators as appointed by King James, were not only very Godly men, they were the most educated and learned men of their day. Once again we will see true Biblical Textual Criticism in action. When you take the time to look at the lives of these men you will discover a group of men with depth and wisdom and men who walked with God. They were the real deal. They were not a bunch of snobby dried up theologians. Many were phenomenal preachers who lead balanced Christian lives and whose lives were living testimonies of the Word of God. They believed in the Doctrine of Divine Inspiration as well as the Doctrine of Divine Preservation. They believed in the inerrant, plenary, verbal, Divine inspiration of the sixty six canonical books of the Old and New Testaments. They believed in the Genesis account of Creation and took God at His Word. They believed in Jesus as the Son of God; His virgin birth; His sinless life; His miracles; His death by the shedding of His blood on the cross; His burial; His physical resurrection and His ascension. They were Godly men, most of whom preached and taught God's plan of salvation at every opportunity. They were pious Protestants who saw through the errors of the Roman Catholic Church. They were Christian scholars of the highest order. Very few scholars today are even close to the depth of scholarship and integrity possessed by these men. It becomes more than obvious, that God had providentially prepared these men for such a task as this.

A few examples of the Translators:

1. John Bois: learned to read Hebrew at age 5; by age 6 he could read and write in the Hebrew language; at 15 he was a student at St. John's College in Cambridge where he was renowned for his grip on the Greek language.

2. Lancelot Andrews: was conversant in 15 languages; referred to as the star of preachers and a great man of prayer possessing a great gulf of learning.

3. Miles Smith: was called a 'Walking Library'; he wrote the 'Preface' for the 1611 KJV; had a deep knowledge of the Greek and Latin fathers; was fluent in Chaldee, Syriac, Arabic, Hebrew and the Ethiopic languages.

4. George Abbot: entered Oxford at age 14 and became the Archbishop of Canterbury

5. Andrew Downes: is described as 'The Chief of the Learned Men of England'

6. Thomas Ravis: became Bishop of London; had many literary accomplishments and was indicative of the entire group of translators: BA1578; MA 1581; BD 1589; DD 1595

7. Dr. John Reynolds: a fellow of Corpus Christi College at age 17; was called "A living Library"; was a master of the Scriptures in the original languages as well as all the ancient records of the church; died during the process and was replaced by John Spencer who as on the Greek Faculty at age 19

8. Richard Brett: proficient in Latin, Greek, Hebrew, Chaldean, Arabic and several Ethiopic tongues; his testimony was one " who was a vigilant pastor, a diligent preacher of God's Word, a liberal benefactor to the poor, a faithful friend and a good neighbour"

9. John Overall: expert in the early church fathers; vital to the translation because of his wealth of knowledge of quotations from the early church fathers

10. John Harding: at the time of his appointment to Translators he had been the Royal Professor of Hebrew in the University for thirteen years

The humility of the Translators is demonstrated in a paragraph in their letter to the reader:

"Truly (good Christian reader) we never thought from the beginning that we should need to make a new translation nor yet to make a bad one a good one,....but to make a good one better, or out of many good ones, one principal good one....... To this purpose there were many chosen, that were greater in other men's eyes than in our own, and though sought the truth rather than their own praise."

They went on to say... "They deserve to be had of us and of posterity in everlasting rememberance.....blessed be they, and most honoured be their name, that break the ice, and give the onset upon that which helpeth forward to the saving of souls."

The Saving of Souls was at the very center of their desire and motivation as Translators of the King James Bible.
The Translators were divided into Six Companies & Assigned to Three Principal Locations:
1. ***Jerusalem Chamber at Westminster***: 10 men under the guide of Lancelot Andrews; Genesis through II Kings and a second company of 7 men under the guide of William Barlow; Romans through Jude
2. ***At Oxford:*** 7 men led by John Harding; Isaiah through Malachi and a Greek Committee of 8 men led by Thomas Ravis; the Gospels, Acts and Revelation
3. ***The Cambridge Groups***: These men dealt exclusively with the Hebrew; Edward Lively led a group of 8 men; I Chronicles through Song of Solomon and 7 men worked with John Bois to translate the Apocrypha

The Translators had to follow 15 Basic Rules:
1. The ordinary Bible read in the Church, commonly called the Bishops Bible, to be followed, and as little altered as the Truth of the original will permit.
2. The names of the Prophets, and the Holy Writers, with the other Names of the Text, to be retained, as nigh as may be, accordingly as they were vulgarly used.

3. The Old Ecclesiastical Words to be kept, viz. the Word Church not to be translated Congregation.
4. When a Word hath divers Significations, that to be kept which hath been most commonly used by the most of the Ancient Fathers, being agreeable to the Propriety of the Place, and the Analogy of the Faith.
5. The Division of the Chapters to be altered, either not at all, or as little as may be, if Necessity so require.
6. No Marginal Notes at all to be affixed, but only for the explanation of the Hebrew or Greek Words, which cannot without some circumlocution, so briefly and fitly be expressed in the Text.
7. Such Quotations of Places to be marginally set down as shall serve for the fit Reference of one Scripture to another.
8. Every particular Man of each Company, to take the same Chapter or Chapters, and having translated or amended them severally by himself, where he thinketh good, all to meet together, confer what they have done, and agree for their Parts what shall stand.
9. As any one Company hath dispatched any one Book in this Manner they shall send it to the rest, to be considered of seriously and judiciously, for His Majesty is very careful in this Point.
10. If any Company, upon the Review of the Book so sent, doubt or differ upon any Place, to send them Word thereof; note the Place, and withal send the Reasons, to which if they consent not, the Difference to be compounded at the general Meeting, which is to be of the chief Persons of each Company, at the end of the Work.
11. When any Place of special Obscurity is doubted of, Letters to be directed by Authority, to send to any Learned Man in the Land, for his Judgement of such a Place.
12. Letters to be sent from every Bishop to the rest of his Clergy, admonishing them of this Translation in hand; and to move and charge as many skilful in the Tongues; and having

taken pains in that kind, to send his particular Observations to the Company, either at Westminster, Cambridge, or Oxford.
13. The Directors in each Company, to be the Deans of Westminster, and Chester for that Place; and the King's Professors in the Hebrew or Greek in either University.
14. These translations to be used when they agree better with the Text than the Bishops Bible: Tyndale's, Matthew's, Coverdale's, Whitchurch's, Geneva.
15. Besides the said Directors before mentioned, three or four of the most Ancient and Grave Divines, in either of the Universities, not employed in Translating, to be assigned by the vice-Chancellor, upon Conference with the rest of the Heads, to be Overseers of the Translations as well Hebrew as Greek, for the better observation of the 4th Rule above specified.

The eighth rule is the one that sets this translation apart from any other. Each one had to separately translate a section and then the whole group would come together and critique the work and agree on what would be accepted. There would therefore be anywhere from 7 to 10 careful revisions to come up with one copy of the text.

The ninth rule would send the completed text to each of the other groups to undergo a critical review by each and every one.

The tenth rule states that if any group finds fault they are to send it back to the original company for another run at it. If the originating company are not in agreement with the suggestions then it goes before a General Committee. This committee is made up of the leaders of all the other companies for a final rendering of the scripture. Therefore, each part of a section of scripture would have been thoroughly gone over at least 14 times.

There is no other Bible like the King James Bible. I believe that God had His 'Providential Hand' on the writing of the KJV and that it is the best English Bible available to man. God in His foreknowledge knew the predominant language in the world would be the English language. There was a time when the sun never set on the English Domain and as a result of this, the Authorized King James Bible was taken around the world. Many of the Puritans and early Christian believers brought the King James Bible to the USA and Canada and it became the foundation for our laws and morality. Two great nations were born and prospered as a result. What a phenomenal Bible!

The King James Bible has stood alone as the number one English Bible for over 400 years.

What about the Apocrypha?

The Apocrypha are not the inspired word of God in any sense whatsoever. Although the Apocrypha (part of the Vaticanus manuscripts) were a part of the Geneva Bible and were included in the Authorized King James Bible of 1611, none of the marginal cross-references to the Apocrypha from the Geneva Bible were included. The Apocrypha was placed between the Old and New Testaments and were never accepted as 'Canon' in the Hebrew Old Testament and were never accepted as 'Canon' in the Greek New Testament. The Apocrypha at best are a collection of ancient literature that the Jewish people looked to for examples of life and instruction in manners. They were full of contradictions and errors and were therefore never considered to be 'Inspired' and were never accepted as 'Canon' by the Church.

Typographical and Grammatical Corrections in the KJV.

By the mid-18th Century it became evident that there were a large accumulation of misprints of the 1611 Authorized King James Version. The Universities of Oxford and Cambridge therefore sought to produce an updated standard text for the

Authorized King James Bible. Since the beginning of the 19th Century, almost all printings of the Authorized King James Version have come from the 1769 Oxford text and have since excluded the Apocrypha all together. Some critics of the KJV point to the typographical errors that were corrected in the 1769 edition as proof that the KJV is a corrupt Bible. However, a typographical error is not a 'scriptural error' but rather it is an error in presentation e.g. the word 'foote' was standardized to 'foot' in the English language in the 19th century and is an example of the minor corrections in the 1769 edition. Not one correction took away from the integrity of the text, nor did it affected any doctrine or precept of the Bible.

Some Christians say that the KJV is too hard to understand... Really?

1 John 5:12
He that hath the Son hath life; *and* he that hath not the Son of God hath not life.
Nineteen one syllable words. Now how difficult is that?

The English of the KJV was not written in the contemporary English used in 1611. If you want to see the contemporary English used in 1611, then get the Translator's Letter to King James and their Letter to the Reader or read 'Foxes Book of Martyrs or the plays of Shakespeare.
The English of the KJV is a Biblical English based on the translation of the Hebrew Text and the Greek Text into an English language that remains true to the language of the God Breathed, Inspired, Original Text; the Word of God. Approximately 90% of Tyndale's Bible was left intact by the King James Translators and Tyndale used an English that even a plough boy would be able to read and understand.
Many modern Biblical textual critics say the KJV should be abandoned because it is not contemporary. However, the

English used in the KJV was never contemporary. It was a Biblical English that rose above the level of daily contemporary speech, and a language which is not only intelligent but also venerable. They also contend that the KJV should be abandoned because of the words 'ye', 'thee', and 'thou'. They believe these words should all be replaced with the word 'you'. The word 'you' is already in the KJV over 950 times in the New Testament alone, but not exclusively. The reason for using 'ye', 'thee', 'thou' was paramount for a true translation of the Original Text into English; 'ye' in the KJV is plural, however, 'thee' is singular. Therefore replacing of the words 'ye', 'thee', and 'thou' with the word 'you' would change the meaning of many verses. These words were needed to maintain a true translation of the Hebrew and Greek language into the exact same meaning in the English language.

Luke 22:31- 32
31. And the Lord said, Simon, Simon, behold, Satan hath desired *to have* you, that he may sift *you* as wheat:
32. But I have prayed for thee, that thy faith fail not: and when thou art converted, strengthen thy brethren.

In these two verses the Lord uses the word 'you' in vs. 31. This is a plural word and indicates that Jesus was addressing all of them. Satan wanted to sift all of them. In vs. 32 the Lord uses the word 'thee' and 'thou'. Jesus was directing this to Simon alone; singular. I have prayed for thee Simon. To replace all these with 'you' would take away from the true and intended message that Jesus was delivering to the group but then in particular to Peter.

Exodus 16:28 (KJV)
And the LORD said unto Moses, How long refuse ye to keep my commandments and my laws?

Exodus 16:28 (NKJV)
And the LORD said to Moses, How long do you refuse to keep my commandments and my laws?

Read these two verses very closely and ask yourself if they both have the same meaning?

Is this a personal chastisement of Moses? Is God asking Moses if he is refusing to keep God's commandments and laws? In this verse it is the people that God is upset with, not Moses. The 'you' in the NKJV, makes it appear that God is reprimanding Moses himself.

The word 'you' can mean both singular and plural in the English language. The 'ye' is a plural word. 'Ye' always means more than one person; plural. Thee, thou, thy, thine, doeth, hast etc. is always a reference to the singular i.e. to one person. The 'y' is plural; Ye... The 't' is singular; Thee.

John 3:7 Marvel not that I said unto thee, Ye must be born again.

Here in *John 3:7,* we have an excellent example of what I am talking about. Jesus is addressing Nicodemus in a personal way; Marvel not that I said unto thee; singular & personal, the 't' is singular and then Jesus says "Ye must be born again" The 'y' is plural; meaning everyone must be born again; plural. There are hundreds of other examples on this issue but this will suffice to help you to understand the necessity of these words.

A Sovereign, Omnipresent, Omniscient, Omnipotent God had providentially protected and preserved His Inspired Word for the Translators in order to give us the beloved King James Bible that we read today.

There is so much more to be said about how we got our Bible but time and space prevent me from going any further.

John Wesley 1703-1791

John Wesley was a celebrated preacher and founder of the Methodist Church who read the Bible in 5 different languages. He was a life-long opponent of the slave trade, who made the following statement........

"I build on no authority, ancient or modern, but the Scripture.

I want to know one thing. The way to Heaven and how to land on that happy shore.

God Himself hath condescended to teach the way. He hath written it down in a book.

O give me that book! At any price, give me that book of God."

John Burgon 1813–1888

John William Burgon was an English Anglican; Dean of Chichester Cathedral in 1876.

He was a defender of the Authorized King James Bible of 1611.

Below are some Burgon quotes that I found on-line.

Burgon Quotes: On Bible Inspiration and against Modern Textual Criticism

"Destroy my confidence in the Bible as an historical record, and you destroy my confidence in it altogether; for by far the largest part of the Bible is an historical record. If the Creation of Man,....the longevity of the Patriarchs, ...the account of the Deluge; ...if these be not true histories, what is to be said of the lives of Abraham, of Jacob, of Joseph, of Moses, of Joshua, of David,... of our Saviour Christ Himself?"

"Will you then reject one miracle and retain another? ... Impossible! You can make no reservation, even in favour of the Incarnation of our Lord, the most adorable of all miracles, as it is the very keystone of our Christian hope."

"Either, with the Best and Wisest of all Ages,... you must believe the Whole of Holy Scripture; ... or... With the Narrow-Minded Infidel... you must Disbelieve the 'Whole'. There is not Middle Course open to you."

What exactly did Burgon believe about the Bible's Inspiration?

"I am asked whether I believe the words of the Bible to be inspired, I answer, To be sure I do, every one of them: and every syllable likewise. Do not you?

Where,....(if it be a fair question,).... Where do you, in your wisdom, stop? The book, you allow, is inspired. How about the chapters? How about the verses? Do you stop at the verses, and not go on to the words? ... No, Sirs! The Bible... (Be persuaded)... is the Very Utterance of the Eternal. As much God's Word, as if High Heaven were open, and We Heard God Speaking to us with Human Voice. Every book of it, is inspired alike; and is inspired entirely. The Bible is none other than the Voice of Him that sitteth upon The Throne. Every Book of it...Every Chapter of it...Every Verse of it... Every Word of it...Every Syllable of it ......(Where are we to stop?) Every letter of it...Is the Direct Utterance of the Most High!

Well spake the Holy Ghost, by the mouth of the many blessed Men who wrote it.

The Bible is none other than the Word of God: Not some part of it, more...Not some part of it, less... but All Alike, The utterance of Him who sitteth upon the Throne... Absolute... faultless ... unerring... supreme!".

John Burgon is perhaps one of the greatest heroes of Biblical Faith and the Verbal Plenary Inspiration and Preservation of Scripture.

Edward F. Hills 1912–1981

Edward F. Hills was one of the greatest 20th Century defenders of the Traditional (Byzantine) Text & Received Text. He was a distinguished Latin and Phi Beta Kappa graduate of Yale University; also earned a Th.B. degree from Westminster Theological Seminary; a Th.M. degree from Columbia Theological Seminary and did doctrinal work at the University of Chicago in New Testament Textual Criticism which he completed at Harvard and in the process earned a Th.D. in this field. He authored a phenomenal book: *'The King James Version Defended'* which outlines six reasons that the King James Bible should be retained. It is an absolute must read. It is thorough and it is deep. It will take a concerted effort on your part to work your way through this book. In the end you will be truly blessed. This book belongs in your library.

Six Reasons the King James Bible should be Retained
(page 218 abbreviated points)

1) "...the English of the King James Version is not the English of the early 17th century. To be exact, it is not a type of English that was ever spoken anywhere. It is biblical English, which...owes its merit, not to 17th-century English — which was very different — but to its faithful translation of the original."

2) "...the King James Version is enduring diction which will remain as long as the English language remains..."

3) "...the current attack on the King James Version and the promotion of modern-speech versions is discouraging the memorization of the Scriptures, especially by children..."

4) "...modern-speech Bibles are unhistorical and irreverent. The Bible is not a modern, human book... On the contrary, the Bible is an ancient, divine Book... Hence the language of the Bible should be venerable as well as intelligible, and the King James Versions fulfills these two requirements better than any other Bible in English."

5) "...modern speech Bibles are unscholarly. The language of the Bible has always savoured of the things of heaven rather than the things of earth. It has always been biblical rather than contemporary and colloquial."

6) "...the King James Version is the historic Bible of English-speaking Protestants. Upon it God, working providentially, has placed the stamp of His approval through the usage of many generations of Bible-believing Christians. Hence, if we believe in God's providential preservation of the Scriptures, we will retain the King James Version, for in so doing we will be following the clear leading of the Almighty."

In language as well as in text the Authorized King James Bible is far superior to any other English translation.

The Translators of our Authorized King James Bible said it best....... "Truly (good Christian reader) we never thought from the beginning that we should need to make a new translation nor yet to make a bad one a good one,....but to make a good one better, or out of many good ones, one principal good one.
And their desire and motivation was to... "give the onset upon that which helpeth forward to the saving of souls."

Chapter Six

OTHER ENGLISH BIBLES AND TRANSLATION COMPARISONS

The Second Stream of English Bibles

We now need to take a look at the *'Second Stream of Bibles'* whose New Testament came out of the Alexandrian Greek Texts of the Vaticanus and the Sinaiticus Documents and whose Old Testament came out of the text called the Leningrad Manuscript (B19a; also called simply L), which was dated around 1008 A.D., and differs widely from the Traditional Hebrew Masoretic Old Testament.

Once we have examined the foundation of this second stream of English Bibles, I would like to compare how they differ from the *'First Stream of Bibles'* whose New Testament came from of the Byzantine Greek Text or the Textus Receptus of the early Apostolic Church and whose Old Testament came from the Hebrew Ben Chayyim Masoretic Text which gave birth to the 1611 Authorized King James Bible.

First we need to look at the two men who were largely responsible for giving us the modern day Bibles that are predicated on the foundation of this second stream of manuscripts.

Who were Westcott and Hort?

Brooks Foss Westcott (1825–1901) was an ordained Anglican Minister and Fenton John Anthony Hort (1828–1892) was a professor at Cambridge University. They are the Fathers of Modern Day Biblical Textual Criticism. The *'Presupposition'* that formed the basis for their Textual Criticism is that the Bible was just another one of the many books from antiquity. To them the Bible was *'just another book'* that was written by man. These are the men who gave us the Revised Version (RV) or sometimes referred to as the English Revised Version (ERV). They completed the New Testament in 1881, the Old Testament in 1885 and the Apocrypha in 1894.

Most if not all of the Modern Day Bibles are based on the 1881 Revised Version of Westcott and Hort. Maybe one of these Modern Bibles is your Bible of choice. It is important for you to know a few things about the men who established the foundation for the Bible that you read.

Westcott and Hort did not believe in the Doctrine of Divine Inspiration nor the Doctrine of Divine Preservation. Does this sound familiar? Both Westcott and Hort rejected the Textus Receptus. Hort referred to it as vile and villainous and believed the Textus Receptus to be both corrupt and perverse. They openly rejected the infallibility of Holy Scripture and refused to acknowledge the authority of the Word of God.

Hort taught that Jesus never claimed to be God himself and just wanted people to see God in him. They believed in Baptismal Regeneration as taught by the Catholic Church i.e. the baptism of babies was their salvation. They taught that the first three chapters of Genesis are pure allegory along with most of the Prophetic Books and portions of the Bible. They did not believe in the history of the Book of Genesis, nor did they believe that Adam and Eve and their descendants were literal historical people. They were followers of Darwin and espoused the theory of Evolution. They rejected the authority of Scripture; they rejected Biblical Salvation; they rejected a real Hell and believed in Purgatory; they constantly referred to Jesus as a created being that needed to be worshipped along with his mother Mary. Much of their theology was Catholic through and through. They were both members of spiritist societies; the Hermes Club and the Ghostly Guild, where they claimed to talk to the spirits of the dead.

All kinds of red flags should be going up at this point but let's continue.

They did not believe in Angels nor the miracles recorded in the Bible. They openly mocked and showed contempt for the great Evangelists of their day; men like Moody and Spurgeon and held exaggerated opinions of their own shallow spirituality. Westcott and Hort were a part of a covert movement within the Anglican Church of England called the **'*Oxford Movement'*.** As members of the 'Oxford Movement' their desire was to usher in a new era of Papal Authority and Catholic Church dominance over the people of England. They believed in the Nicolaitan Higher-Archie of the Catholic Church: Pope, Cardinals, Priests and all the pageantry and ritualism associated with it. Apparently they did not understand &/or believe in the scripture of *Revelation 2:6*.

Revelation 2:6
But this thou hast, that thou hatest the deeds of the Nicolaitans, which I also hate.

In all of the various articles that I have read on the life and habits of both Westcott and Hort, they never one time proclaimed nor indicated that they were saved by Grace through Faith in Jesus Christ. They were textual critics of the worst kind. They were wolves in sheep's clothing who were considered to be the intellectual giants within the Church of England and yet they did not believe in the Scriptural Authority of the Bible and were actively working to bring down the very Church they represented. To accomplish this task, they first had to destroy the foundation upon which the Protestant Church of England rested; the Authorized 1611 King James Bible, and replace it with a new Bible i.e. the Revised Bible of 1881.

Let me ask you again; upon which stream of Bibles does your Bible of choice rest?

The Revised Bible of Westcott & Hort
This version was the joint effort of the Universities of Oxford and Cambridge, and had its origin in an action taken by the Convocation of the Province of Canterbury in February 1870. Brooke Foss Westcott (Regis professor of Divinity at Cambridge), and Fenton John Anthony Hort (Lecturer on New Testament at Cambridge), were put in charge of this project. The Convocation of Canterbury laid down some basic rules which were to be observed by the translation groups.

These rules were as follows:
1. To introduce as few alterations as possible into the text of the Authorised Version.
2. To limit, as far as possible, the expression of such alterations to the language of the Authorized and earlier English Versions.
3. Each company to go twice over the portion to be revised, once provisionally, the second time finally, and on principles of voting as hereinafter is provided.
4. That the Text that is to be adopted be that for which the evidence is decidedly preponderating; and that when the Text so adopted differs from that from which the Authorised Version was made, the alteration be indicated in the margin.

5. To make or retain no change in the Text on the second final revision by each Company, except **two thirds of those present** approve of the same, but on the first revision to decide by simple majorities.
6. In every case of proposed alteration that may have given rise to discussion, to defer the voting thereupon till the next meeting, whensoever the same shall be required by **one third of those present** at the meeting, such intended vote to be announced in the notice for the next meeting.
7. To revise the headings of chapters and pages, paragraphs, italics, and punctuations.
8. To refer, on the part of each Company, when considered desirable, to Divines, Scholars, and Literary Men, whether at home or abroad, for their opinions.

In addition to the rules just mentioned, the Convocation also passed five resolutions that were to govern the actions of the translation Committees.

These resolutions are as follows:
1. That it is desirable that a revision of the Authorised Version of the Holy Scriptures be undertaken.
2. That the revision be so conducted as to comprise both marginal renderings and such emendations as it may be found necessary to insert in the text of the Authorised Version.
3. That in the above resolutions we do not contemplate any new translation of the Bible, or any alteration of the language, except where in the judgment of the most competent scholars such change is necessary.
4. That in such necessary changes, the style of the language employed in the existing Version be closely followed.
5. That it is desirable that Convocation should nominate a body of its own members to undertake the work of

revision, who shall be at liberty to invite the cooperation of any eminent for scholarship, to whatever nation or religious body they may belong.

Once the process was set in motion, it did not take long for Westcott and Hort to show their true colours. They were not about to follow any of the Rules or Resolutions as set out by the Convocation of Canterbury. They had no intention of revising the 1611 Authorized King James Bible as instructed, but rather, they determined to replace it with a New Bible based on the Alexandrian Vaticanus and the Sinaiticus manuscripts.

<u>The Foundation for the Greek New Testament of Westcott & Hort</u>

As I mentioned before the Roman Emperor Constantine (306 -377) was responsible for giving the Catholic Church the *Eusebio-Origen Bible*. From this Bible came the *Greek Vaticanus MS or the Codex B* and the *Greek Sinaiticus or Codex Aleph.* In Latin they had the Vulgate (which was changed or corrupted) into the *Latin Bible of Jerome,* from which came the English translation of the *Douay-Rheims Bible:* the New Testament was translated at the English College at Rheims in 1582 while the Old Testament was translated into English by the English College at Douay in 1609. The Douay-Rheims Bible was greatly influenced by both Greek documents of the Vaticanus and Sinaiticus. In English they also had the *Jesuit Bible of 1582,* which also went through some vast changes in order to line up with the Douay-Rheims Catholic Bible. It is this *Second Stream of Bibles* that gave birth to the *1881 Revised Bible.* To come up with a new 'New Testament' in the English language that would be sympathetic to the Catholic Church, Westcott and Hort had to by necessity, reject the *Textus Receptus* and the thousands of Greek MSS that served as the foundation for the Authorized King James Bible of 1611. They authored their own Greek Text based on the Greek documents of the Vaticanus and Sinaiticus which would later be revised to the Nestles-Aland and the UBS Greek Texts both of which maintained the essence of the Alexandrian Manuscripts.

As covert members of the 'Oxford Movement' it was their goal and their mission to put together an English Bible that would help to Romanize the people of England once again.

Old Testament of Westcott & Hort

For the Old Testament, Westcott and Hort rejected the Ben Chayyim Masoretic Text used for the 1611 King James Bible and used instead the Ben Asher text. This text was based on a text called the Leningrad Manuscript (B19a; also called simply L), which was dated around 1008 A.D., and differs widely from the Traditional Hebrew Masoretic Old Testament.

The Ben Asher text is exhibited in Rudolf Kittel's Biblia Hebraica (BHK, 1937) with all of his suggested footnote changes, as well as in the Stuttgart edition of Biblia Hebraica (BHS, 1967-77) with all of their suggested footnote changes. Both of these texts offer in their footnotes about fifteen to twenty suggested changes per page (changes from the authentic Ben Chayyim Masoretic text). This adds up to about 20,000 to 30,000 changes in the entire Hebrew Old Testament text.

The Old Testament of the 1881 Revised Version is the source of the Old Testament translations for most of the modern bible versions today. Read the introductory pages in the front of your Bible to find out where it fits; is it part of the First Stream or the Second Stream?

Unlike the Translators of the KJV, Westcott and Hort put together only two committees to oversee this entire endeavour. These committees would meet in secret behind closed doors. Together Westcott and Hort ran rough shod over anyone and everyone who opposed any of their theological positions on this project. To the shame of this committee, Westcott and Hort even included a Unitarian pastor Dr. Vance Smith. Unitarianism is a religious theological movement named for its understanding of God as one person, in direct contrast to the Doctrine of the Trinity. To the Unitarian, Jesus was a prophet, and in some sense the "son" of God, but not God himself. Westcott and Hort not only allowed this man on their Bible Committee, they also allowed him to partake in Communion with the committee.

The only two shining stars in this committee were John Burgon and Dr. Scrivener. Both these men fought tooth and nail with Westcott and Hort concerning the changes they were making to the KJV but to no avail. Burgon and Scrivener were of the same mindset as the Translators of the 1611 Authorized King James Bible. They were godly men who believed in the Doctrines of Divine Inspiration and Preservation and were committed to limiting the changes to the Authorized KJV to grammatical and spelling corrections, however, they were constantly out manoeuvred, over ruled and out voted by the rest of the committee over which Westcott and Hort had complete control.

Westcott and Hort also had a second Revision Team in the United States which was as corrupt as the one in England. When the Committee in England finished a certain portion of the Revised Bible, they would send it to the committee in the USA to review, however, this USA committee were never allowed to actively participate in any discussions and were excluded from any input as Westcott and Hort held an iron fist over all the procedures on both sides of the Atlantic.

It should also be noted that the American Revision team were forced by Westcott and Hort into an agreement to wait a full 20 years before publishing this new Bible in the United States (it was all about the money; money was more important to them than souls) the American Standard

Version (ASV) was therefore published by the Thomas Nelson Publishers in 1901.

Sad to say the same can be said of many of today's new modern Bibles; it is all about the money. Most of the modern day Bibles (NIV, ESV, ASV, NASV, NKJV etc.) have already had several revisions themselves and this translates into more money.

With very few exceptions, most of the new modern day bibles have as their foundation the Greek Text of Westcott and Hort for their New Testament and the corrupted Ben Asher Texts and the Septuagint for their Old Testaments. Therefore the same problems that exist between the Authorized 1611 King James Version and the 1881 Revised Version are also prevalent with all of the modern day bibles as well.

For Westcott and Hort to call their Bible the 'Revised Bible' is a misrepresentation of the truth. The 1881 Revised Bible is not a 'Revision'. They did not in any shape or form revise the KJV or any other English Bible available to them. The 1881 Revised Bible is a new Bible based on a completely different family of manuscripts, texts, and documents. It is in essence a Catholic Bible that has its origin and it's foundation in this *Second Stream of Bibles*.

Comparison: Authorized King James Bible 1769 vs. the 1881Revised Version:

I want to show some comparisons of scripture between these the two Streams of Bibles. We will compare the King James Bible with the Catholic Douay-Rheims Bible, the Revised Version along with some of the modern day Bibles that came as a result of the corrupt Biblical Textual Critics of Westcott & Hort.

We will compare the following Bibles:
1. Authorized King James Version (KJV) – *Benjamin Blayney Oxford 1769 edition*

2. Douay-Rheims Bible (DRB) – *Catholic Bible (NT 1582 – OT1609)*
3. Revised Version (RV) – *Westcott & Hort (1881-1894)*
4. New International Version (NIV) – *(2011 Biblica inc.)*
5. English Standard Version (ESV) – *(Text Edition 2011 Good News Publishers)*
6. New King James Version (NKJV) – (1982 Thomas Nelson)
7. New American Standard Bible (NASB) – (1995 update Lockman Foundation)

I want to demonstrate a few examples of the scriptural problems between the Authorized KJV and the Bibles listed above. Unfortunately a new Bible and/or a revision of a new Bible comes out in print just about every year, so these examples are only a few of the Bibles on the market today. I firmly believe that many of these new Bibles are in direct violation of the warnings as found in *Deuteronomy 4:2* and *Revelation 22: 18 – 19*.

We live in perilous times and we have a tremendous need to hear and understand the Truth of God's Word as it was handed down to man by the very Breath of God.

Matthew 6:13
KJV: And lead us not into temptation, but deliver us from evil: For thine is the kingdom, and the power, and the glory, for ever. Amen.
DRB: And lead us not into temptation. But deliver us from evil. Amen.
RV: And bring us not into temptation, but deliver us from the evil *one*.
NIV: And lead us not into temptation but deliver us from the evil one.
ESV: And lead us not into temptation, but deliver us from evil.

Other English Bibles and Translation Comparisons

NKJV: And do not lead us into temptation, But deliver us from the evil one.

NASB: And do not lead us into temptation, but deliver us from [a]evil.
[b][For Yours is the kingdom and the power and the glory forever. Amen.']

NASB Foot Note: [a] or the evil one [b] this clause not found in early mss

*Look at the change in the Lord's Prayer; the deleting of most of the verse and in the RV adding the **"evil one"**. How did Satan get into the Lord's Prayer?* **Note:** *the NIV and the NKJV are word for word with the RV and the ESV is word for word with the DRB; the NASB agrees with these in the Foot Notes. Let us remember that, the kingdom, the power and the glory belong to God for ever. It is thought that the Church at Rome wanted the power and the glory to go to the Church and have therefore deleted that section from the Lord's Prayer.*

The KJV never leaves the issue about the supremacy of God in question.

Matthew 5:44
KJV: But I say unto you, Love your enemies, bless them that curse you, do good to them that hate you, and pray for them which despitefully use you, and persecute you;

DRB: But I say to you, Love your enemies: do good to them that hate you: and pray for them that persecute and calumniate you:

RV: but I say unto you, Love your enemies, and pray for them that persecute you;

NIV: But I tell you, love your enemies and pray for those who persecute you,

ESV: But I say to you, Love your enemies and pray for those who persecute you,

NKJV: But I say to you, love your enemies, bless those who curse you, do good to those who hate you, and pray for those who spitefully use you and persecute you,[a]
Foot note [a]NU-Text omits three clauses from this verse, leaving, *"But I say to you, love your enemies and pray for those who persecute you."*
NASB: But I say to you, love your enemies and pray for those who persecute you,

*Please note that **"bless them that curse you"** was omitted in the DRB and the RV. This is a direct result of the influence of the Vaticanus and the Sinaiticus manuscripts. This demonstrates that the RV is not a Revision of the KJV but rather a New Bible based on a different family of Greek MSS. Modern Day Bibles such as the ESV, the NIV (and others; ASV, NASB, NKJV etc.) owe all or much of their translation to the RV Version which basically falls in line with the Catholic Douay-Rheims Bible and the Vaticanus and Sinaiticus manuscripts.*

Luke 2:33

KJV: And Joseph and his mother marvelled at those things which were spoken of him.
DRB: And his father and mother were wondering at those things which were spoken concerning him.
RV: And his father and his mother were marveling at the things which were spoken concerning him;
NIV: The child's father and mother marveled at what was said about him.
ESV: And his father and his mother marveled at what was said about him.
NKJV: And Joseph and His mother[a] marveled at those things which were spoken of Him.
Foot Note: [a] NU-Text reads *And His father and mother.*
NASB: And His father and mother were amazed at the things which were being said about Him.

This is a very subtle attempt to take away from the Virgin Birth and the Deity of Jesus when they make reference to Joseph as the father of Jesus. Note: the NKJV has Joseph as the father in the footnotes!

<u>Luke 4:8</u>

KJV: And Jesus answered and said unto him, Get thee behind me, Satan: for it is written, Thou shalt worship the Lord thy God, and him only shalt thou serve.
DRB: And Jesus answering said to him. It is written: Thou shalt adore the Lord thy God, and him only shalt thou serve.
RV: And Jesus answered and said unto him, It is written, Thou shalt worship the Lord thy God, and him only shalt thou serve.
NIV: Jesus answered, "It is written: 'Worship the Lord your God and serve him only.'
ESV: And Jesus answered him, "It is written, "'You shall worship the Lord your God, and him only shall you serve.'"
NKJV: And Jesus answered and said to him, "Get behind Me, Satan![a] For[b] it is written, 'You shall worship the LORD your God, and Him only you shall serve.'
Footnotes: [a] NU-Text omits *Get behind Me, Satan*. [b] NU-Text and M-Text omit *For*.
NASB: Jesus answered him, "It is written, 'You shall worship the Lord your God and serve Him only.'

Some believe that the Church in Rome wanted **'Get thee behind me, Satan'** *dropped from this scripture verse. The Lord used this same expression when dealing with Peter in Matthew 16:23 and the Catholic Church did not want to put the apostle Peter on the same level as Satan.*

Most of the modern day Bibles fall in line with the DRB and the RV or have indicated such in their Foot Notes as in the NKJV.

Luke 11: 2-4
KJV:
2. And he said unto them, When ye pray, say, Our Father which art in heaven, Hallowed be thy name. Thy kingdom come. Thy will be done, as in heaven, so in earth.
3. Give us day by day our daily bread.
4. And forgive us our sins; for we also forgive every one that is indebted to us. And lead us not into temptation; but deliver us from evil.

DRB:
2. And he said to them: When you pray, say: Father, hallowed be thy name. Thy kingdom come.
3. Give us this day our daily bread.
4. And forgive us our sins, for we also forgive every one that is indebted to us. And lead us not into temptation.

RV:
2. And he said unto them, When ye pray, say, Father, Hallowed be thy name. Thy kingdom come.
3. Give us day by day our daily bread.
4. And forgive us our sins; for we ourselves also forgive every one that is indebted to us. And bring us not into temptation.

NIV:
2. He said to them, "When you pray, say: "'Father, hallowed be your name, your kingdom come.
3. Give us each day our daily bread.
4. Forgive us our sins, for we also forgive everyone who sins against us. And lead us not into temptation."

ESV:
2. And he said to them, "When you pray, say: "Father, hallowed be your name. Your kingdom come.
3. Give us each day our daily bread,
4. and forgive us our sins, for we ourselves forgive everyone who is indebted to us. And lead us not into temptation."

NKJV:
2. So He said to them, "When you pray, say: Our Father in heaven,[a]Hallowed be Your name. Your kingdom come.[b] Your will be done On earth as *it is* in heaven.

Footnotes: [a] NU-Text omits *Our* and *in heaven*. [b] NU-Text omits the rest of this verse.

3. Give us day by day our daily bread.
4. And forgive us our sins, For we also forgive everyone who is indebted to us. And do not lead us into temptation, But deliver us from the evil one.

NASB:
2. And He said to them, "When you pray, say: '[a]Father, hallowed be Your name. Your kingdom come.

Footnotes: [a] Later mss add phrases from Matt 6:9-13 to make the two passages closely similar

3. 'Give us each day our daily bread.
4. 'And forgive us our sins, For we ourselves also forgive everyone who is indebted to us. And lead us not into temptation.'"

The DRB, the RV and other Modern Day Bibles like the NIV and the ESV have cut out, 'Our Father which art in heaven' and 'Thy will be done, as in heaven, so in earth'. This is a subtle attack on the authority of God in both heaven and earth. Once again Satan gets mention in the Lord's Prayer in Luke 11: 4 of the NKJV?

<u>Acts 16:7</u>
KJV: After they were come to Mysia, they assayed to go into Bithynia: but the Spirit suffered them not.
DRB: And when they were come into Mysia, they attempted to go into Bithynia: and the Spirit of Jesus suffered them not.
RV: and when they were come over against Mysia, they assayed to go into Bithynia; and the Spirit of Jesus suffered them not;

NIV: When they came to the border of Mysia, they tried to enter Bithynia, but the Spirit of Jesus would not allow them to.
ESV: And when they had come up to Mysia, they attempted to go into Bithynia, but the Spirit of Jesus did not allow them.
NKJV: After they had come to Mysia, they tried to go into Bithynia, but the Spirit[a] did not permit them.
Footnotes: [a] NU-Text adds *of Jesus*.
NASB: and after they came to Mysia, they were trying to go into Bithynia, and the Spirit of Jesus did not permit them;

The replacement of the 'Spirit' with the 'Spirit of Jesus' is a complete misrepresentation of the Third Person of the Trinity, the 'Holy Spirit'. There are a lot of people who do not believe in the Person of the Holy Spirit and these changes to Acts 16:7 fall in line with those incorrect teachings. Note the Foot Note in the NKJV.

1 Corinthians 5:7

KJV: *Purge out therefore the old leaven, that ye may be a new lump, as ye are unleavened. For even Christ our passover is sacrificed for us:*
DRB: *Purge out the old leaven, that you may be a new paste, as you are unleavened. For Christ our pasch is sacrificed.*
RV: *Purge out the old leaven, that ye may be a new lump, even as ye are unleavened. For our passover also hath been sacrificed, even Christ:*
NIV: *Get rid of the old yeast, so that you may be a new unleavened batch—as you really are. For Christ, our Passover lamb, has been sacrificed.*
ESV: *Cleanse out the old leaven that you may be a new lump, as you really are unleavened. For Christ, our Passover lamb, has been sacrificed.*
NKJV: *Therefore purge out the old leaven, that you may be a new lump, since you truly are unleavened. For indeed Christ, our Passover, was sacrificed for us.*[a]

Footnotes: [a] NU-Text omits for us.
NASB: Clean out the old leaven so that you may be a new lump, just as you are in fact unleavened. For Christ our Passover also has been sacrificed.

*The DRB, the RV and the Modern Day Bibles take away the words- sacrificed **"for us"**. This is a subtle strike against the atonement. The atonement is the center of the entire Gospel and the KJV makes it very clear who our sacrifice is and that the sacrifice was **"for us"**.*
They say that the KJV is difficult to understand – I find the verse in the DRB to be more than difficult to understand and the foot note in the NKJV is unacceptable.

1 Corinthians 15:47
KJV: The first man *is* of the earth, earthy: the second man *is* the Lord from heaven.
DRB: The first man was of the earth, earthly: the second man, from heaven, heavenly.
RV: The first man is of the earth, earthy: the second man is of heaven.
NIV: The first man was of the dust of the earth; the second man is of heaven.
ESV: The first man was from the earth, a man of dust; the second man is from heaven.
NKJV: The first man *was* of the earth, *made* of dust; the second Man *is* the Lord[a] from heaven. Footnotes: [a] NU-Text omits *the Lord*.
NASB: The first man is from the earth, earthy; the second man is from heaven.

*Only the KJV is clear as to who the second man from heaven is; '**the Lord from heaven**'. Again the footnote in the NKJV casts doubt on this Scripture verse.*

Ephesians 3:9

KJV: And to make all *men* see what *is* the fellowship of the mystery, which from the beginning of the world hath been hid in God, who created all things by Jesus Christ:

DRB: And to enlighten all men, that they may see what is the dispensation of the mystery which hath been hidden from eternity in God who created all things:

RV: and to make all men see what is the dispensation of the mystery which from all ages hath been hid in God who created all things;

NIV: and to make plain to everyone the administration of this mystery, which for ages past was kept hidden in God, who created all things.

ESV: and to bring to light for everyone what is the plan of the mystery hidden for ages in God who created all things,

NKJV: and to make all see what *is* the fellowship[a] of the mystery, which from the beginning of the ages has been hidden in God who created all things through Jesus Christ;[b]

Footnotes: [a] NU-Text and M-Text read *stewardship* (dispensation). [b] NU-Text omits *through Jesus Christ*

NASB: and to bring to light what is the administration of the mystery which for ages has been hidden in God who created all things;

*Here we see a very subtle attack on the Deity of Christ. The DBR, the RV and many of the Modern Day Bibles take away from the fact that Jesus Christ is the **Creator God**. They also missed the 'fellowship of the mystery'. This is the fellowship that God the Father, God the Son and God Holy Spirit enjoyed before the foundation of the world. Only the KJV brings out the fullness of this wonderful relationship while unfortunately the NKJV once again adds a foot note that casts doubt and confusion.*

Colossians 1:14

KJV: In whom we have redemption through his blood, *even the forgiveness of sins:*
DRB: In whom we have redemption through his blood, the remission of sins:
RV: in whom we have our redemption, the forgiveness of our sins:
NIV: in whom we have redemption, the forgiveness of sins.
ESV: in whom we have redemption, the forgiveness of sins.
NKJV: in whom we have redemption through His blood,[a] the forgiveness of sins.
Footnotes: [a] NU-Text and M-Text omit *through His blood*.
NASB: in whom we have redemption, the forgiveness of sins.

This is a direct attack on the doctrine of **redemption through his blood.** *The omission of these words can be traced back to Origen (200AD) who expressly denies that the body and the soul of our Lord was offered as the price of our redemption. Eusebius was a devoted follower of Origin who edited the Vatican Manuscript and* **"through his blood"** *was deleted from the Vulgate. However, the Douay-Rheims Bible from which documents the RV relied heavily on for their translation has this translation correct. Therefore this was a deliberate change of scripture on the part of Westcott and Hort in the Revised Version. Many Modern Day Bibles followed the lead of the Revised Version and have cut out the reference to* **'redemption through his blood'** *as well.*

This change alone should make any Bible believing born-again Christian put away the Modern Day Translations and return to the Authorize King James Bible. Notice the Foot Note of the NKJV as it once again throws doubt on the true and trusted Word of God.

1 Timothy 3:16

KJV: And without controversy great is the mystery of godliness: God was manifest in the flesh, justified in the Spirit, seen of angels, preached unto the Gentiles, believed on in the world, received up into glory.

DRB: And evidently great is the mystery of godliness, which was manifested in the flesh, was justified in the spirit, appeared unto angels, hath been preached unto the Gentiles, is believed in the world, is taken up in glory.

RV: And without controversy great is the mystery of godliness; He who was manifested in the flesh, justified in the spirit, seen of angels, preached among the nations, believed on in the world, received up in glory.

NIV: Beyond all question, the mystery from which true godliness springs is great: He appeared in the flesh, was vindicated by the Spirit, was seen by angels, was preached among the nations, was believed on in the world, was taken up in glory.

ESV: Great indeed, we confess, is the mystery of godliness: He was manifested in the flesh, vindicated by the Spirit, seen by angels, proclaimed among the nations, believed on in the world, taken up in glory.

NKJV: And without controversy great is the mystery of godliness: God[a] was manifested in the flesh, Justified in the Spirit, Seen by angels, Preached among the Gentiles, Believed on in the world, Received up in glory.

Footnotes: [a] NU-Text reads *Who*.

NASB: By common confession, great is the mystery of godliness: He who was revealed in the flesh, Was vindicated in the Spirit, Seen by angels, Proclaimed among the nations, Believed on in the world, Taken up in glory.

Again we see an outright attack on the Deity of Christ. While the KJV points out that **'God was manifest in the flesh'**, *The DRB, the RV and many of the Modern Day Bibles* *toke out the word '**God**' and replace it with '**He who**'. Once again the NKJV has a confusing foot note.*

Hebrews 7:21
KJV: (For those priests were made without an oath; but this with an oath by him that said unto him, The Lord sware and will not repent, Thou *art* a priest for ever after the order of Melchisedec:)
DRB: But this with an oath, by him that said unto him: The Lord hath sworn and he will not repent: Thou art a priest for ever).
RV: (for they indeed have been made priests without an oath; but he with an oath by him that saith of him, The Lord sware and will not repent himself, Thou art a priest for ever);
NIV: but he became a priest with an oath when God said to him: "The Lord has sworn and will
not change his mind: 'You are a priest forever.'
ESV: but this one was made a priest with an oath by the one who said to him: "The Lord has sworn and will not change his mind, 'You are a priest forever.'"
NKJV: (for they have become priests without an oath, but He with an oath by Him who said to Him: "The LORD has sworn And will not relent, 'You *are* a priest forever[a] According to the order of Melchizedek'")
Footnotes: [a] NU-Text ends the quotation here.
NASB: (for they indeed became priests without an oath, but He with an oath through the One who said to Him, "THE LORD HAS SWORN AND WILL NOT CHANGE HIS MIND, 'YOU ARE A PRIEST FOREVER'")

*The DRB, the RV and many other Modern Day Bibles omit '**after the order of Melchisedec**'. Again this is a subtle attack on the deity of Jesus Christ. He is a Prophet; a Priest and a King and to take away the reference to '**after the order of Melchisedec**' is a vain attempt at taking away the* *cross-reference between the Old Testament and the New Testament Melchisedec and all the scriptural lessons that we can draw from this. As you can see the NKJV has a dubious foot note once again concerning this issue.*

<u>Revelation 22:14</u>
KJV: Blessed *are* they that do his commandments, that they may have right to the tree of life, and may enter in through the gates into the city.
DRB: Blessed are they that wash their robes in the blood of the Lamb: that they may have a right to the tree of life and may enter in by the gates into the city.
RV: Blessed are they that wash their robes, that they may have the right *to come* to the tree of life, and may enter in by the gates into the city.
NIV: "Blessed are those who wash their robes, that they may have the right to the tree of life and may go through the gates into the city.
ESV: Blessed are those who wash their robes, so that they may have the right to the tree of life and that they may enter the city by the gates.
NKJV: Blessed *are* those who do His commandments,[a] that they may have the right to the tree of life, and may enter through the gates into the city.
Footnotes: [a] NU-Text reads *wash their robes*.
NASV: Blessed are those who wash their robes, so that they may have the right to the tree of life, and may enter by the gates into the city.

*The DRB and the RV have changed this verse from '**do his commandments**' to '**wash their robes in the blood of the Lamb**'? Again this demonstrates that the Revised Version was a new Bible translation and not a '**revision**' of the KJV. Again we see the Modern Day Bibles lining themselves up with the DRB and the RV, with the NKJV lining itself up in the footnotes?*

These few comparisons should be sufficient to show you the glaring differences between the Authorized King James Bible and the Revised Version which is the foundation for most of the Modern Day Bibles that followed. Which Stream of Bibles does your Bible of choice line itself up with?

The Authorized King James Bible stands alone and should be the Bible of choice for Christians who hunger and thirst for Truth of the Word of God.

Who Killed Goliath in Your Bible? II Samuel 21:19
Most modern day Bibles condemn themselves. Thank God for giving us the wisdom to determine His infallible words from the words of men.

KJV: *"Elhanan...slew the brother of Goliath."*
DRB: " *Adeodatus... slew Goliath the Gethite*
RV: *"Elhanan...slew Goliath the Gittite."*
NIV: *"Elhanan...killed Goliath the Gittite."*
ESV: *"Elhanan...killed Goliath the Gittite."*
NKJV: *"Elhanan...killed Goliath the Gittite."*
NASB: *"Elhanan...killed Goliath of Gath."*

As you see from this simple test, only one of these Bibles tells the truth about Goliath and Elhanan. We all learned at a young age in Sunday school that David killed Goliath. (I Sam. 17). The Holy Spirit tells us plainly that Elhanan, one of David's chosen men, killed Lahmi, the brother of Goliath (I Chron. 20:5). The King James Bible had this scripture correct way back in 1611?

I am reading a rather interesting book whose author is using the *NKJV* as his reference guide. When he came to this verse in II Samuel 21:19 he made the comment that this had to be another person called Goliath? Had he used the KJV, this comment would not have been necessary as he would have had the truth i.e. Elhanan slew the brother of Goliath.

What's New about the New King James Bible?

The NKJV was largely the work of about 130 Bible scholars and the Thomas Nelson publishers. In fact the leading Baptist Pastor that I made mention of in Chapter 3, was a major player in the scripting of the NKJV. When I discovered this, it became apparent to me why he condemned as heretics, those of us who believe the Authorized KJV to be the Inspired and Preserved Word of God. This group of scholars advertised the NKJV as the 'Fifth Edition' of the Authorized KJV, which of course it is not.

What is wrong with the New King James Version? All it does is modernize the words of the Authorized King James Bible....right? This could not be farther from the truth.

The publishers of the NKJV laid claim that they used the Textus Receptus Greek New Testament of the Authorized KJV, however this is only a half truth and a half truth is really a half lie. Some of them held to the Textus Receptus and some of them held to the Greek texts of Westcott and Hort (Nestle-Aland/UBS Greek Texts). Neither of the two groups believed that God had protected and preserved the 'Original Inspired Manuscripts'. They believed that over time and at the hands of man, the Originals were corrupted and therefore contain errors. In the translation of the NKJV they have in essence changed thousands of words, ruined valuable verses, and when not agreeing with the King James Bible, they have lined themselves up with the DRB, RV, NIV, NASB or the RSV.

Changed Words Means Changed Meanings
Acts 3:25- 26 (KJV)
25. Ye are the children of the prophets, and of the covenant which God made with our fathers, saying unto Abraham, And in thy seed shall all the kindreds of the earth be blessed.

26. Unto you first God, having raised up his **Son** Jesus, sent him to bless you, in turning away every one of you from his iniquities.

Acts 3:25-26 (NKJV)
25. You are sons of the prophets, and of the covenant which God made with our fathers, saying to Abraham, 'And in your seed all the families of the earth shall be blessed.
26. To you first, God, having raised up His **Servant** Jesus, sent Him to bless you, in turning away every one *of you* from your iniquities."

Do you see a difference between these two Bible versions?

In the Authorized KJV, we find that Jesus is God's Son.

In the NKJV, we find that Jesus is God's servant.

The Greek word found in the text here is "pais". It can be used in Greek for either "son" or "servant." It is important therefore to look at the context in order to come to the correct word. The passage is talking about "children," and "fathers" and "seed." The ***New King James*** translators chose "***servant.***" Why? They were not alone. The New World Translation, created by the Jehovah's Witnesses who deny the deity of Jesus, translated this word "servant" as well as the NIV, ASV, NASV and many other modern Bible translations.

They refused to translate the word as "son" in this powerful sermon where Peter presents Jesus as the Messiah and the Son of God. If they had used the Textus Receptus as their foundation for the writing of the NKJV then the word 'son' would have been used in this verse.

The NKJV has ignored the KJV Greek Textus Receptus over 1200 times and as mentioned in Chapter Four, the NKJV has replaced the 'thee', 'ye', 'thou' of the KJV with the word 'you' which will change the meaning of many verses of scripture. The NKJV has also replaced the trusted Old Testament

Hebrew Ben Chayyim Masoretic Text with the very corrupt Ben Asher Hebrew Bible.

The NKJV is a poor attempt at replacing the real deal in the Authorized KJV.

The NKJV logo that you see here is the ancient symbol for the pagan trinity. It is a symbol used by the Masons for the Royal Arch (Lucifer) of the 3rd Degree York Order of Masonry and is also displayed on the albums of rock groups like Led Zeppelin and incorporated on some of the New Age literature. It is not a symbol that should appear on the Word of God.

Is the NKJV a Bible that we can trust with our eternal destiny? Or is it just another one of the many modern day translations that are causing confusion within our Bible Churches today?

Jeff Foxworthy is a well know comedian.
He is famous for his 'You might be a Red Neck' jokes and even a few Canadian jokes.
If you ever cut your grass and find a car... You might be a Red Neck!
If you have to move the transmission so your wife can take a bath.... You might be a Red Neck!
If your dog and your wallet both have the same chain... You might be a Red Neck!
If you know all 4 seasons:
Almost winter, winter, still winter and road construction... You might be Canadian!
If you have more miles on your snow blower than on your car... You might be Canadian!
If you find 2 degrees "a little chilly"... You might be Canadian!

And I say..........
If your Bible takes away from the Deity of Christ..........You might have the Wrong Bible!
If your Bible takes away or adds to the Word of God......You might have the Wrong Bible!
If your Bible tells you that Elhanan slew Goliath...........You might have the Wrong Bible!
If your Bible takes away from the blood of Christ..........You might have the Wrong Bible!

We need to make sure that our Bible of Choice is God's Bible of choice.
Which Bible do you believe Jesus would recommend?

Deuteronomy 4:2
Ye shall not add unto the word which I command you, neither shall ye diminish *ought* from it, that ye may keep the commandments of the LORD your God which I command you.

Chapter Seven

WHAT MUST I DO TO BE SAVED?

Acts 16:30
And brought them out, and said, Sirs, what must I do to be saved?

Acts 16:31
And they said, Believe on the Lord Jesus Christ, and thou shalt be saved, and thy house.

Here in Acts chapter 16, we find Paul and Silas in jail in the city of Philippi. An Angel has just loosed their bonds and the jailer was ready to fall on his sword when Paul prevented him. In total despair the jailer throws himself before Paul and Silas and desperately asked the most important question in the entire Bible………***Sirs, what must I do to be saved?***

Acts 16:30 presents a simple question and *Acts 16:31* provides a simple answer; or does it? It is the most important question that anyone could ever ask and upon the answer to this question hangs the eternal destination of our 'Soul'.

First and foremost we need to know God's Mindset on Salvation.

2 Peter 3:9
The Lord is not slack concerning his promise, as some men count slackness; but is longsuffering to us-ward, not willing that any should perish, but that all should come to repentance.

According to *2Peter 3:9*, God is not willing that anyone should perish. That is God's will. That is His mindset. God's desire is that all should come to repentance. He does not want anyone to perish and spend eternity separated from Him in Hell.

What then must I do to be saved?
Before we can deal with the question of salvation, we have to deal with the question of 'Faith'. Faith is the key that unlocks the Door to Salvation.

Hebrews 11:6
But without faith *it is* impossible to please *him:* for he that cometh to God must believe that he is, and *that* he is a rewarder of them that diligently seek him.

The Bible is clear......"without faith it is impossible to please Him".

What then is Faith?

Hebrews 11:1
Now faith is the substance of things hoped for, the evidence of things not seen.

First and foremost our position on Faith must be Biblical. Our faith in God is not to be based on some arbitrary whim or some random thought process. Without faith we will have no true understanding of God, of His Person, of His truth, of His wisdom, or of His promises. Our Faith is crucial and absolutely necessary to establish an honest and living relationship with a real and living God.

Hebrews 11 pays tribute to many Old Testament heroes of faith such as Noah, Abraham, Sarah, Joseph, Moses etc. God spoke directly to these Old Testament saints and they all died in faith, not having received the promises. They saw them a far off, and because of God's Grace and through Faith, they were persuaded of them and embraced them even though they confessed that they were strangers and pilgrims on the earth.

Faith is one of those words that is difficult to tie down to one simple definition. Some teach that faith is a belief system that does not require proof or evidence. This definition of faith is simply not true. This kind of faith will not unlock the Truth of God's Word and will not allow you to understand who God is. Faith is not the opposite of fact, nor is it the opposite of scientific knowledge. Many Christians will give *Hebrews 11:1* as their definition of faith and just leave it at that. However, a person would need to know what faith is before *Hebrews 11:1* would make much sense. When teaching the Word of God, I like to use the *'kiss'* method: *'keep it simple stupid'*. The 'stupid', would of course, be a reference to myself, so please do not get offended with the acronym.

My 'kiss' definition of faith would be this: 'take God at His Word'.

This definition may be too simplistic for the sophisticated theology of the so called intellectual critics but the fact still remains, our faith is to be centered in God and anchored in His Word. This is why it is so critical to have the correct Bible. A Bible that will give you God's clear, concise and accurate description of who He is. Your eternal destiny rests on a Faith that is predicated on the Word of God and without which you cannot please God.

Romans 10:17
So then faith cometh by hearing and hearing by the word of God.

Why take a chance with a Bible whose foundation rests on corrupt manuscripts and was written by men who do not believe in the Biblical Doctrines of Inspiration and Preservation. Is your Bible of choice God's Bible of choice for you? Think about it. Do you know the God you believe in and more importantly does He know you? Do you have an intimate relationship with Him and does He have one with you? You will never achieve a clear understanding of who He is apart from true Biblical faith.

Biblical Faith is not Wishful Thinking.

Biblical Faith is having full confidence in God's Word. Biblical Faith accepts God's word as *fact* and acts accordingly. There are many evidences that the Word of God is true. Our Faith is not to be some kind of Kierkegaard existential leap into the unknown that teaches faith, in its most commonly used meaning, is the act of believing in or accepting something intangible or unprovable, or without empirical evidence. This is the position held by many of the humanistic textual critics and the foundation upon which they operate; men like Westcott and Hort. God has never expected us to leap into the unknown. God has given man His inspired, inerrant Word that openly tells us who He is; I AM. Here I AM in the words of My Book. Biblical Faith is to be an intelligent and thoughtful acceptance of the wondrous words of the great I AM.

Pastor David Reagan from the Antioch Baptist Church in Knoxville Tennessee has a wonderful article on faith in which he gave the three aspects of faith as established by the Reformers of the sixteenth and seventeenth centuries.

The Three Aspects of Faith:
1. Knowledge
Faith begins with a knowledge of what it is that should be believed. For instance, if someone knows that the gospel of Christ refers to the death, burial, and resurrection of Christ according to the scriptures as found in, 1 Corinthians 15:1-4, then they have ***knowledge***. However, it is possible for someone to know what the gospel is without believing it to be true. Therefore Knowledge is not enough.

2. Assent
The person must also believe that the object of his faith is true. To reach this level of faith, the person must know what the gospel is (Knowledge) and believe it to be true (assent). But this is still not enough for salvation. This takes us to the third aspect of faith.

3. Trust
Trust refers to a personal commitment to and reliance upon an object of faith. In salvation, the sinner must know that Jesus died for him and rose again from the dead (***knowledge***) and he must accept that these facts are true (***assent***). However, he is still not saved until he relies (***trust***) on these facts as the basis for his personal salvation.

Pastor Reagan used the following example of these three aspects of Faith: "Let us say that you are visiting someone's home and they ask you to sit down. First you look over and acknowledge that there is indeed a chair: ***This is Knowledge***. Second you accept the fact that you could sit in this chair and that it would hold you up: ***This is Assent***. Finally, you walk over to the chair and you sit down: ***This is Faith***. You exercised your faith in the chair when you sat down".

2 Corinthians 5:7 (For we walk by faith, not by sight:)

We are to live our life in such a way that the words of God are fully accepted and serve as the foundation and direction for our lives. We must walk the walk and talk the talk. Any faith not founded on the true and inspired Word of God is not Biblical Faith, it is superstition at best. Faith is taking God at His Word.

My oldest son and I have had many challenging conversations concerning spiritual matters. It is always a good thing to have someone who can challenge you on your Biblical positions. Sometimes we agree and sometimes we do not, but these spiritual sword drills have always forced me to look deeper into the Word of God and for this I am very thankful. He sent me this description of 'Faith' as presented by C.H. Spurgeon.

C. H. Spurgeon 1834–1892

C. H. Spurgeon was a British Baptist Preacher; he was to 19th Century England what D. L. Moody was to America. Spurgeon was known as the Prince of Preachers and he had an amazing description of what Faith is.

Lectures Delivered before the Young Men's Christian Association in Exeter Hall 1858-1859

"Our faith is a person;
The gospel that we have to preach is a person;
Go wherever we may, we have something solid and tangible to preach
For our gospel is a person.
If you had asked the twelve Apostles in their day,
'What do you believe in?'
They would not have stopped to go round about with a long sermon,
They would have pointed to their Master
They would have said........'We believe him.'
'But what are your doctrines?'
'There they stand incarnate.'
'But what is your practice?'
'There stands our practice.............. He is our example.'
'What then do you believe?'
Hear the glorious answer of the Apostle Paul,
'We preach Christ crucified.'
Our creed, our body of divinity,
Our whole theology is summed up in the person of Christ Jesus."
"Our faith is a person"

And I would add that this 'Person' is the Word of God and we need to take Him at His Word.

If God is not willing that we should perish..........What then is His Plan to prevent this?

What must we do to be saved? (Acts 16:30)

This question is a two pronged question.
1. What then is Salvation?
2. What must I do to get Salvation?

If *Faith* is taking God at His Word, then according to God's Word*: **What is Salvation?***

First and Foremost Salvation is all about God's Grace.
God's Word tells us how Salvation is achieved; by grace through faith alone.

Ephesians 2:8-9
8. For by grace are ye saved through faith; and that not of yourselves: *it is* the gift of God:
9. Not of works, lest any man should boast.

Ephesians 4:7
But unto every one of us is given grace according to the measure of the gift of Christ.

Noah Webster 1828 Dictionary: definition of Grace: the free unmerited love of God; the spring and source of all the benefits men receive from Him (Rom 11:6) ; a state of reconciliation with God (Rom.5:2); through God's Grace we have access by faith into the grace wherein we stand.

Everything we have is because of God's Grace.....His unmerited love. God's unmerited favour towards man is a *free gift* and everyone "is given grace according to the measure of the gift of Christ"....God's Son.

John 3:16
For God so loved the world, that he gave his only begotten Son, that whosoever believeth in him should not perish, but have everlasting life.

Our Grace comes from the Father through His Son (Ephesians 4:7) and each individual gets enough Grace for the purpose for which God has designed us. We are made in the image and likeness of God and we were designed for the sole purpose of spending eternity with Him.

God is not willing that any man should perish and to this end and for this purpose, through an expression of His love and an extension of His Grace, God gave us His Son.

Jesus is a gift. God's Inspired Word is a gift. God's love is a gift. All this because of God's gift of Grace; the free unmerited love of God. Our Salvation is available to us through an act of God's Grace. We don't deserve it and we cannot work for it. Apart from God there is nothing within the heart of man that is righteous enough or good enough to earn our salvation.

Romans 12:3
For I say, through the grace given unto me, to every man that is among you, not to think *of himself* more highly than he ought to think; but to think soberly, according as God hath dealt to every man the measure of faith.

Here in *Romans 12:3* the Bible is telling us that God has given to everyman a measure of faith or rather 'the measure of faith'.

The Bible also tells us in the Gospel of John that God has shed the true 'Light' on every man that comes into the world.

John 1:9
That was the true Light, which lighteth every man that cometh into the world.

What Must I do to be Saved?

Psalms 119:130
The entrance of thy words giveth light; it giveth understanding unto the simple.

God also demonstrates who He is through His Creation.

Romans 1:20
For the invisible things of him from the creation of the world are clearly seen, being understood by the things that are made, *even* his eternal power and Godhead; so that they are without excuse:

So let's look at the Gifts that God has given to man.
1. Gift of His Inspired Word – the Bible (2Pet.1:20-21, 2Tim.3:16)
2. Gift of Grace – (Ephesians.4:7 – though the Gift of His Son)
3. Gift of His Son – (John 3:16)
4. Gift of Faith – (Romans 12:3)
5. Gift of Light (knowledge) – (John 1:9, Psalms 119:130)
6. Gift of Creation – (Romans1:20)

Now we need to examine another important Gift from God.
When God breathed the breath of life into Adam and Adam became a living soul, he was also given a 'Free Will'. Like Adam, we are free agents in God's Universe. God has given every man a 'Free Will' and with this 'Free Will' comes not only the freedom but also the responsibility to make life choices. Our 'Free Will' is another one of God's unmerited acts of love towards us. Our Free Will is another extension of His Grace. Therefore when it comes to Salvation, we have a choice to make and every choice we make comes with a consequence: either good or bad.

In light of all the Gifts that God has given to man, what then are His expectations?

God's will is that everyone should come to the point of salvation and to this end and for this purpose, God has given to each of us His inspired Word along with enough *'Grace'* and enough *'Faith'* and enough *'Light'* to make an intelligent decision concerning Salvation. God's desire is for us to take Him at His Word and to take our gift of *'Faith'* and *'willingly'* place this gift of faith into His Son Jesus Christ.

Unfortunately, many will put their faith into the Church, or into some unbiblical spiritual experience or into some form of secular humanism trusting in self. They will disregard the gifts that God has provided and will exercise their free will to live their lives separated from God and spiritually dead in their trespasses and sin.

How would you explain who Jesus is?

If you were asked to explain what you mean when you say 'I am a Christian'. What would you say? Many people would say, "I believe in Jesus", but then so do the devils.

James 2:19

Thou believest that there is one God; thou doest well: the devils also believe, and tremble.

Have you ever been confronted by a Jehovah's Witness? They believe in Jesus and they will tell you that they are Christians. What would the Jehovah's Witness tell you about their Jesus? Their 'New World Translation Bible' says; "In the beginning was the Word and the Word was with God and the Word was a god". They would tell you that Jesus is 'a god' but not Jehovah God. They would tell you that Jesus is dead and that He is in a grave somewhere and that his body is not decaying. Do you think that their Jesus is our Jesus?

What would the Mormon's tell you about Jesus? They believe in Jesus and they would also tell you that they are Christians as well. They would tell you that Jesus is the

Son of God. The Mormons teach that there are trillions of planets ruled by millions of Gods who were once humans like us. These millions of gods had many wives and one of these Mormon gods gave birth to a spirit child named Elohim. Somehow he was later born to humans who gave him a physical body and that through obedience to Mormon teaching and his death and resurrection, Elohim proved himself worthy and was elevated to God Hood like his father before him. Mormons believe that Elohim is their heavenly father and that he lives on a planet with his many wives and together they had millions of spirit children who would be sent to earth and that Jesus and Lucifer were two of the spirit children of Elohim; they were brothers.

Lucifer rebelled and took one third of the spirit children with him; Devil and Demons. Those who followed the Mormon Jesus were given human bodies. They were white skinned and called Delightsome in the Mormon Bible. The Mormons teach that Adam and Eve were actually Elohim and one of his goddess wives. Later in history Elohim came to Mary and had a physical relationship with her and Jesus who was the Spirit Child of Elohim, received his human body and then later Jesus took three wives, Mary, Martha and Mary Magdalene. The Mormon Trinity consists of: Joseph Smith, Elohim and Jesus. The Mormons will tell you that they believe in Jesus. Do you think that their Jesus is our Jesus?

2 Peter 2: 1–2

1. But there were false prophets also among the people, even as there shall be false teachers among you, who privily shall bring in damnable heresies, even denying the Lord that bought them, and bring upon themselves swift destruction.
2. And many shall follow their pernicious ways; by reason of whom the way of truth shall be evil spoken of.

I have many loved ones and some very good friends who are living lives outside of the will of God. I wish it were not so, but sadly it is. The Lord is standing there with open arms and a kind tender heart begging them to come to Him.

Matthew 7:13-14
13. Enter ye in at the strait gate: for wide *is* the gate, and broad *is* the way, that leadeth to destruction, and many there be which go in thereat:
14. Because strait *is* the gate, and narrow *is* the way, which leadeth unto life, and few there be that find it.

A person that desires to come to God, must understand and believe in who He is *(knowledge)* and then he must believe that He will do what He has promised *(assent)* and then he must go by faith and place his complete and total trust in Him and Him alone *(trust)*..........*this is Faith and this is Salvation!*

How could a person ever get to the point of salvation without true Biblical Faith that...."cometh by hearing and hearing by the word of God"? *(Romans 10:17)*

Hebrews 11:6
But without faith *it is* impossible to please *him:* for he that cometh to God must believe that he is……………………..

Who then is Jesus?
As a Christian I believe in the ***Biblical Jesus*** as found in the Bible. In the event that I haven't made it clear, my Bible of choice is the Cambridge Authorized King James Bible 1769 edition, which I believe to be the verbal, plenary, inspired Word of God. It is my Final Authority and my only Authority for who Jesus is; for who God is. This Bible is a book in which the fullness of God has been revealed to man. God is saying "Here I AM". I AM right here in the

pages of this Book from Genesis to Revelation. God's Word instructs us to look at His Creation. *(Romans 1:20)* Creation is physical proof of a Creator God; of the Great I AM. God is saying that Creation is proof of who He is: look at all of my planets, all my stars, the solar systems, planet earth and the amazing abundance of life; look at all this and know that I AM. My son sent me a powerful little vignette concerning God's name 'I AM'.

"I was regretting the past and fearing the future when suddenly my Lord was speaking:

My name is I AM
He paused.
I waited.
He continued.
When you live in the past with its mistakes and regrets it is hard. I am not there.
My name is not I WAS.
When you live in the future, with its problems and fears, it is hard. I am not there.
My name is not I WILL BE.
When you live in this moment, it is not hard. I am here.
My name is I AM."

Exodus 3:14
And God said unto Moses, I AM THAT I AM: and he said, Thus shalt thou say unto the children of Israel, I AM hath sent me unto you.

Open your Bible to *Job 38:1* and read the conversation that God had with Job. It is an amazing discourse on who God is.

The Bible tells us that the Godhead consists of a Trinity; God the Father, God the Son and God the Holy Spirit. They are Eternal, no beginning, no ending, Alpha and Omega. They enjoyed a wonderful loving relationship before Creation. The

Bible does not say that they created man because they were lonely or unhappy or unfulfilled. God's desire, God's will and God's mindset is for us to be with Him in Heaven and for us to enjoy the fellowship of the God Head. This is God's express purpose for the Creation of Man.

Revelation 4:11
Thou art worthy, O Lord, to receive glory and honour and power: for thou hast created all things, and for thy pleasure they are and were created.

John 17:24
Father, I will that they also, whom thou hast given me, be with me where I am; that they may behold my glory, which thou hast given me: for thou lovedst me before the foundation of the world.

John 14:1-3
1. Let not your heart be troubled: ye believe in God, believe also in me.
2. In my Father's house are many mansions: if *it were* not *so*, I would have told you. I go to prepare a place for you.
3. And if I go and prepare a place for you, I will come again, and receive you unto myself; that where I am, *there* ye may be also.

1Corinthians 2:9
But as it is written, Eye hath not seen, nor ear heard, neither have entered into the heart of man, the things which God hath prepared for them that love him.

Jesus wants us to spend eternity with Him. He want us to see Him high and lifted up in all of His glory and wants us to see and to understand the fullness of the Trinity and the relationship that they shared before the foundation of the world. The question is, do you want to be there? Do you want to share in everything that God has prepared for you?

Nothing takes God by surprise. He is Omniscient. God knew that man was going to break God's Law. He knew that man would fall from his initial created state of perfection into a very imperfect state of sin. God also knew that because of this, sin would enter into the world and be passed on to all succeeding generations of man.

Romans 5:12
Wherefore, as by one man sin entered into the world, and death by sin; and so death passed upon all men, for that all have sinned:

Therefore, before creation and before the foundation of the world, the Godhead made a very important executive decision. Together they came up with God's Plan of Salvation &/or God's Plan of Redemption.

So what is God's Plan of Redemption for our Sin?
Ezekiel 18:4
……the soul that sinneth, it shall die.

Romans 6:23
For the wages of sin *is* death……….

Man because of his sin and in accordance to God's Law deserves to die. The price on our sin is death. This death is not an instant physical death; it's a spiritual death that separates man from God. When sin entered into the world it killed us spiritually and it is killing us physically. What do you think 'Old Age' is all about? We were not designed to grow old and get sick.

As I sit here writing this book, I am thinking of my cancer, my diabetes and the numerous eye operations to stop the bleeding, the replacement operation for my left knee, the pains in my shoulders from the numerous sports related separations, pins put in and pins taken out. People tell me that I am in my 'Golden Years'......Really!? Hey, I am just getting old. My 'Golden Years' were back when I was eighteen to twenty years old and on top of my game! Getting old, getting sick, the plumbing wearing out sucks, but it is something we all go through: it is just a part of the process that entered into the world because of sin. It is a confirmation that sin has entered into the world and death by sin. Sin has killed us spiritually and is in the process of killing us physically. Sin has condemned man to a life separated from God. If we die physically and enter eternity spiritually separated from God, our sin will take us to Hell and God's Law will be satisfied.

In God's Plan, however, Jesus agreed to step out of heaven and become a man. *(John 1:14)* Jesus would then live that perfect sinless life that we were designed to live. He would live a life in complete and total compliance with God's Law and God's Standards and maintain a consistent, continuous loving relationship with the Father. He was sinless and therefore uniquely qualified to die in man's place, in my place. The innocent, sinless Lamb of God would die by the shedding His blood on the cross and thereby redeem my Soul from the depths of Hell. His plan of Redemption was to pay the debt that I owe for my sin. This Plan was not some arbitrary random act of God that came as the result of being caught off guard by our sin. This was a Plan that was thoughtfully predetermined and agreed upon by the God Head well before the foundation of the world. Before God ever created a thing, we were on his mind. (*1Peter 1:20, Revelation 13:8*)

God's Plan of Salvation is a wonderful example of God's Mercy and God's Grace.

The late Lester Rolof has a great sermon on line called Dr. Law & Dr. Grace. It is an entertaining message from a great man of God. Lester Rolof was known for putting the jam on the bottom shelf so that people like myself could reach it and enjoy it. This message is a wonderful and colourful lesson on how Dr. Law brings the lost sinner to Dr. Grace and this is a lost teaching in many Christian circles today. It is the Law that leads a lost person to Jesus.

In light of what God has done......what then must we do to be saved?
I have heard people say things like 'God's Simple Plan of Salvation'. However, God's Plan is really not that Simple. *Salvation is personal.* His death was sufficient to cover the Sin of the World, but Salvation is about the individual and each individual must make their own personal decision and this takes us back to the beginning of this chapter.

First I Must believe that HE IS...This is a Must.

Hebrews 11:6 ... for he that cometh to God must believe that he is.........

Who then is Jesus?

The Doctrine of the Trinity is a Must Believe.
I must believe that Jesus is God; that He is part of the Godhead; part of the Trinity. When an individual comes to God, he or she is coming to 'God the Father', 'God the Son' and 'God the Holy Spirit'. This is who God is. This is who our Jesus is; He is God the Son.

1 John 5:7–8
7. For there are three that bear record in heaven, the Father, the Word, and the Holy Ghost: and these three are one.
8. And there are three that bear witness in earth, the Spirit, and the water, and the blood: and these three agree in one.

The Virgin Birth of Jesus is a Must Believe
We must believe that through an operation of the God Head, Jesus was born of the Virgin Mary. He was not just a man that rose up to become God. He is God who stepped down from His thrown in Glory to become Flesh and to dwell among us.

Matthew 1:23
Behold, a virgin shall be with child, and shall bring forth a son, and they shall call his name Emmanuel, which being interpreted is, God with us. (Isaiah 7:14)

Hebrews 2:16–17
16. For verily he took not on *him the nature of* angels; but he took on *him* the seed of Abraham.
17. Wherefore in all things it behoved him to be made like unto *his* brethren, that he might be a merciful and faithful high priest in things *pertaining* to God, to make reconciliation for the sins of the people.

John 1:14
And the Word was made flesh, and dwelt among us, (and we beheld his glory, the glory as of the only begotten of the Father,) full of grace and truth.

1 Timothy 3:16 ... God was manifest in the flesh, justified in the Spirit, seen of angels, preached unto the Gentiles, believed on in the world, received up into glory.

Jesus is All God and All Man; God Manifest in the Flesh; The Son of God and God the Son.
The Virgin Birth of Jesus was a demonstration of the Trinity in action.

Luke 1:34–35
34. Then said Mary unto the angel, How shall this be, seeing I know not a man?
35. And the angel answered and said unto her, The Holy Ghost shall come upon thee, and the power of the Highest shall overshadow thee: therefore also that holy thing which shall be born of thee shall be called the Son of God.

Joseph is not the father of Jesus. Jesus is the Son of God. If your Bible of choice tells you that Joseph was the father of Jesus then you have the wrong Bible.

Luke 2:33 KJV
And Joseph and his mother marvelled at those things which were spoken of him.

Luke 2:33 RV
And his father and his mother were marveling at the things which were spoken concerning him;

Most modern Bibles; RV, NIV, ESV, DRB show Joseph as His father. The NKJV has it in the footnotes! What's up with that nonsense?

The Sinless Life of Jesus is a Must Believe
The entire Bible talks about a Holy God, a Pure God, a Righteous God, a God who is without sin. Jesus never one time committed a sin, he never one time thought a sinful thought nor committed a sinful act. He is pure; He is righteous and He is without sin because He is God.

2 Corinthians 5:21
For he hath made him *to be* sin for us, who knew no sin; that we might be made the righteousness of God in him.

The fact that We are Sinners is a Must Believe.
Many theologians do not believe in Sin nor a literal Hell. Many today will only talk about the fact that God is love. This is where the Law of God is so important. It reveals the purity and Holiness of God and at the same time reveals the depravity of man's heart.

Jeremiah 17:9
The heart *is* deceitful above all *things,* and desperately wicked: who can know it?

The very reason for God's Law is to bring a person to the realization that we are indeed sinners in need of a Saviour and the Bible is clear on the subject of sin and its consequences.
The Law holds us by the hand and leads us to the Door..... that would be Jesus! *(John10:7-9)*.

Galatians 3:24
Wherefore the law was our schoolmaster *to bring us* unto Christ, that we might be justified by faith.

It all started with Adam's sin of disobedience in the Garden of Eden and there is not a person who can escape the consequences of Adam's fall.

Romans 5:12
Wherefore, as by one man sin entered into the world, and death by sin; and so death passed upon all men, for that all have sinned:

Romans 3:10
As it is written, There is none righteous, no, not one:

Romans 3:23
For all have sinned, and come short of the glory of God;

We were made in the image and likeness of God and we were created to be eternal beings. We have a Body, a Soul and a Spirit. The Soul is who we are and is the center of our mind, our will and our emotions. Our Soul lives within our Body and our Body is that part of us that allows our Soul to express itself and communicate with man. The Spirit is that part of us that allows our Soul to communicate with God and our Spirit lives within our Soul. I know this is a very simple description but it works. *(kiss)*

Every one of us have sinned. We have sinned in our actions, in our words and in our thoughts...we have broken God's Law. The Bible tells us that we all have that sin that does so easily beset us. *(Hebrews 12:1)* Sin is a part of the inherent nature that was passed down to us from Adam. We do not have to teach our children to lie....this is something that comes to them without any instruction from Mom or Dad and because of sin our Spirit died. That part of us that enables our Soul to communicate with God is dead. The unsaved person today is just a "Dead Man Walking". Our Rebellious Sinful Nature has separated us from God, it killed us spiritually and continues to kill us physically.

Not only are we sinners; There is a Price that must be paid. God's Law must be satisfied.

Ezekiel 18:4
......the soul that sinneth, it shall die.

Romans 6:23
For the wages of sin *is* death...........

Wages are something that we earn. At the end of a pay-period we get our wages. We have worked for them and we deserve to get them.

I have often heard people who are frustrated and upset with God when going through difficult times say things like "God is not fair". However, I am glad that God is not fair. If God were fair then I would get what I deserved and I would die separated from God because of my sin and I would rightfully and justifiably go to a place prepared for the Devil and his angels and thereby satisfy God's law in a place called Hell.

We must see ourselves as Sinners in need of a Saviour, in need of Redemption, in need of Salvation. We also have to understand that it is because of our sin that we are in this mess!

My preacher has a very appropriate statement on sin:
1. Sin will take you farther than you ever wanted to go
2. Sin will keep you longer than you ever wanted to stay
3. Sin will cost you more than you ever wanted to pay

Hebrews 9:27
And as it is appointed unto men once to die, but after this the judgment:

We have an appointment with God and we will have no excuse when we stand in front of Him ……………*and stand in front of Him we will!*

The question we need to ask ourselves is this; 'How am I going to get out of this mess?'
Because of my sin, I will come face to face with the living God who knows every detail of my life. This will not be a conversation about my good works out weighing my bad works. This will be a conversation about my sin. There is nothing within myself that will satisfy God's Law, other than my eternal separation from God in Hell. I have put myself

into a situation from which it is humanly impossible to escape and I have no one to blame but myself.

The late Robert G. Lee has a famous sermon called 'Payday Someday', if you have never heard this sermon then Google it; it is an absolute must hear.

We are in a hopeless situation from which we cannot save ourselves......But God has a Plan!

Acts 4:12
Neither is there salvation in any other: for there is none other name under heaven given among men, whereby we must be saved.

John 14:6
Jesus saith unto him, I am the way, the truth, and the life: no man cometh unto the Father, but by me.

Jesus was crucified on the Cross. He Shed His Blood. He died.
Hebrew 9:22
................without shedding of blood is no remission.

Romans 5: 8- 9
8. But God commendeth his love toward us, in that, while we were yet sinners, Christ died for us.
9. Much more then, being now justified by his blood, we shall be saved from wrath through him.

In *Titus 3:7* we were justified by his Grace and now in *Romans 5:9* we are justified by His Blood. Through the Shedding of His Blood and His death on the cross, Jesus paid in full for all our sin and freely offers a way of escape from God's wrath; from God's judgement.

What can wash away my sins – nothing but the blood of Jesus.

He took our place; He took my place. He died on the cross, was buried and His soul descended into Hell where He satisfied God's Law on my behalf. Three days later He physically arose from the dead and walked out of His tomb. What an awesome God!

Hebrews 2:9
But we see Jesus, who was made a little lower than the angels for the suffering of death, crowned with glory and honour; that he by the grace of God should taste death for every man.

This is God's Plan of Redemption. Only a kind tender compassionate God would come up with a Plan and then freely provide everything we need to enter into it.

Romans 6:23
For the wages of sin *is* death; but the gift of God *is* eternal life through Jesus Christ our Lord.

What can man do to earn his Salvation or his Redemption?
The answer to this question is simple; Nothing! The gift of God is eternal life! Everything has been done for us by The God Head. They have done it all, it is Finished, it is Complete; it is a free Gift and it is Recorded in His Book.

Titus 3:5
Not by works of righteousness which we have done, but according to his mercy he saved us......

Mercy is the ultimate demonstration of God's Grace through His son Jesus. Mercy is another gift from a Gracious God, which in itself incorporates the Gift of Forgiveness. Mercy and Forgiveness are symbiotic gifts that feed off one another and are absolutely two of the most essential ingredients of God's Plan of Salvation. Jesus paying the Price for our Sin is an example of both the Grace and Mercy of a God that is not willing that any should perish. It is a Divine expression of His true love and compassion. It shows the depth of the love of God, in that He was willing to place His only begotten Son into the hands of sinful men that He might be slain, and thus redeem us from eternal sorrow. No other god among all the gods in this world has ever come close to the kind of God we serve.

Noah Webster 1828 Dictionary states:

Mercy is benevolence, mildness or tenderness of heart which disposes a person to overlook injuries, or to treat an offender better than he deserves; to forgive trespasses and injuries.

Grace is God's unmerited favour; giving us something that we do not deserve....Salvation. Mercy is God's tenderness of heart; not giving us something that we do deserve....Hell.

Our God is the true and living God. He is a kind, tender, compassionate God who has borne our grief's and carried our sorrows.

Isaiah 53:4–5
4. Surely he hath borne our griefs, and carried our sorrows: yet we did esteem him stricken, smitten of God, and afflicted.
5. But he *was* wounded for our transgressions, *he was* bruised for our iniquities: the chastisement of our peace *was* upon him; and with his stripes we are healed.

We owed a debt of sin that we could not pay. Jesus paid for a debt of sin that He did not owe. We are unrighteous wicked sinners at the best of times and we do not deserve the Grace and the Mercy that our Lord has extended to all who will accept it. Salvation is all His doing; it is all about Him and this takes us to another Must Believe.

The Resurrection of Jesus from the Grave is a Must Believe.
Jesus shed His blood and died on the cross. He was buried and 3 days later He rose from the Dead.

Romans 10:9
That if thou shalt confess with thy mouth the Lord Jesus, and shalt believe in thine heart that God hath raised him from the dead, thou shalt be saved.

I love Easter. I love the Song, 'Up from the Grave He Arose'.

1 Corinthians 15: 55–57
55. O death, where *is* thy sting? O grave, where *is* thy victory?
56. The sting of death *is* sin; and the strength of sin *is* the law.
57. But thanks *be* to God, which giveth us the victory through our Lord Jesus Christ.

The stone was rolled away. His dead body came back to life. Jesus stood up. With His nailed scared hands He folded and laid aside His grave clothes and with His nailed scared feet He physically walked out of the Tomb. His resurrection is real and recorded in the Bible.

> Living He loved me
> Dying He saved me
> Buried He carried my sins far away
> Rising He justified freely forever
> One day He's coming – oh glorious day!

If you have one of the modern day Bibles, will you look at *1 Corinthians 15:55* and then tell me that they have not changed the meaning of this verse concerning the resurrection from the "grave". The Modern Day Bible replaces 'O grave' with 'O death'. This is a very subtle attack on a very important truth in the Word of God. Many cults do not believe in the bodily resurrection of our Saviour, so they spiritualize the resurrection or cut out the reference of His resurrection from the "grave".

The Authorized King James Bible is always very clear on Biblical Truth.

We have a Choice to make.
The Stage has been set and God has provided everything we need in order for us to make an intelligent and an appropriate decision about who He is and what we must do to be saved.

We must come to God with a Repentant Heart.

2 Peter 3:9
The Lord is not slack concerning his promise, as some men count slackness; but is longsuffering to us-ward, not willing that any should perish, but that all should come to repentance.

2 Corinthians 7:10
For godly sorrow worketh repentance to salvation not to be repented of………..

Noah Webster 1828 Dictionary: Repent – to remember with sorrow
Repentance – the sorrow for anything done or said; the pain or grief which a person experiences in consequence of the injury or inconvenience produce by his own conduct.
Repentance is a lost teaching in many of today's Churches and yet it is an essential part of God's Plan of Salvation. Many people will admit that they are sinners, but they really do not want to turn from sin. They enjoy their sin. They

may feel guilty for their sin, but many only show sorrow when they get caught. Some will even say a "Jesus" prayer and for a short time their conscience is cleared, however, they simply continue with their life style with no evidence of repentance. They will not repent; they will not turn; they will not Trust in God's Plan of Salvation. This is the essence of a confessional at the Catholic Church. Some of the most difficult people to get saved are religious people like the Anglicans and the Catholics. I can pick on these because I was an Anglican and my wife was a Catholic. There is enough scripture in the Apostles' Creed and the Nicene Creed for anyone to get saved, however, for most of us this was all just head knowledge. As an Anglican I had the head knowledge concerning the Trinity but I had no heart knowledge. When it came to Salvation it was difficult for me to see my need. I was ok. I was like so many of my family and friends. I was baptised and confirmed. My wife was baptised and confirmed and went to a Catholic School right up to high school. We got married in the Anglican Church only because I got into an argument with my wife's Catholic Priest who insisted that I become Catholic and/or for me to sign an agreement promising to raise our children in the Catholic Church. He then threatened to excommunicate my wife if I didn't agree to his conditions and because she had not been in regular attendance he wanted her to pay some back-tithes...really... think about it ... come on really... he had just threatened to excommunicate my future wife... I am Irish and I was a Protestant and Oh yes, he had just stepped on my fighting side. At this point the meeting was over. I was so upset with this arrogant little man I was shaking. I stood up and leaned forward and looked him straight in the eye. He sat motionless and was visibly taken back. It wouldn't be polite to tell you what I said to him but it ended with, "you don't have the authority to excommunicate anyone', and we left. Needless to say we got married at St. Paul's Anglican Church.

I knew that I was a sinner. No one had to convince me of that, but I was ok. I was covered by my Church, by my Baptism, by my Confirmation. I took communion every time I was in Church. I was just as good as the person sitting beside me and I enjoyed my life style. I was living large and enjoying life as I knew it. I had absolutely no idea what Biblical Salvation was all about. I thought it was the Church and that is where my faith was, in my Church.

Salvation; Not so simple is it?

Jesus made many Choices on Our Behalf

Jesus did not have to go to the Cross for us. Going to the Cross was His Choice and His Desire and a part of His Plan of Salvation.

Matthew 26:53
Thinkest thou that I cannot now pray to my Father, and he shall presently give me more than twelve legions of angels?

We have to understand who we are. We are Sinners. We have broken God's Law. There is a Price on our Sin. The Wages of sin is death. Because of our Sin we are separated from God and on our way to Hell. We are in a mess that we cannot humanly escape from and we have put ourselves there. We must turn from our sin and with a repentant heart we must ask for Forgiveness. We must take the gift of Faith and put our Faith and Trust into God's Plan of Salvation. We must put our faith into Jesus Christ and His finished work on the cross. We must open our mouth and personally invite Jesus into our hearts as our Lord and our Saviour.

Romans 10:10
For with the heart man believeth unto righteousness; and with the mouth confession is made unto salvation.

Romans 10:13
For whosoever shall call upon the name of the Lord shall be saved.

John 1:12
But as many as received him, to them gave he power to become the sons of God, *even* to them that believe on his name:

1John4 5:12
He that hath the Son hath life; *and* he that hath not the Son of God hath not life.

You have a Choice to make .... and only you can make it.... this is personal.
Over the course of our lives we are faced with thousands upon thousands of choices. However, when it comes to eternity there are only two choices that we can make.

Will you accept God's Plan of Salvation?
Will you chose life and spend eternity with God in Heaven?
……………..Or…………………..
Will you reject God's Plan of Salvation?
Will you chose death and spend eternity separated from God in Hell?

Ezekiel 18:32
For I have no pleasure in the death of him that dieth, saith the Lord GOD: wherefore turn *yourselves*, and live ye. (Repent)

Isaiah 45:21- 23
21. Tell ye, and bring *them* near; yea, let them take counsel together: who hath declared this from ancient time? *who* hath told it from that time? *have* not I the LORD? and *there is* no God else beside me; a just God and a Saviour; *there is* none beside me.

22. Look unto me, and be ye saved, all the ends of the earth: for I *am* God, and *there is* none else.
23. I have sworn by myself, the word is gone out of my mouth *in* righteousness, and shall not return, That unto me every knee shall bow, every tongue shall swear.

What could possibly prevent you from bowing your head in prayer and doing your part in God's Plan of Salvation? What is stopping you?

Prayer is simply talking to God. You need to take care of business. You need to make a Choice. This is personal. You have your Free Will and enough knowledge to make the right decision. Just get it done. Pray from your heart to the heart of God. He is waiting for you with open arms. There is no sin – no matter how vile or how many – that He is not willing and ready to forgive and forget. He can wipe the slate clean and He desires to give you a new lease on life.

You can do this. Take God at His Word and put your faith and trust into Jesus.

Below is a suggested prayer, however, you can pray your own prayer. He knows your heart.

Dear Lord
I know that I am a sinner and I understand that my sins have separated me from You
I Believe in Jesus Christ; God the Son; Who became flesh through the virgin birth
I Believe in His finished work on the Cross
I Believe that He willingly died in my place to satisfy God's Law on my behalf
I Believe that He shed His blood to pay the full price for my Redemption
I Believe that He was buried and three days later He arose from the Dead

I ask you to forgive me of my sin and to have mercy on me a sinner
By God's Grace I am placing my faith and my complete trust into Jesus Christ the Son of God
I ask Jesus Christ to come into my heart as my Lord and my Saviour
I trust Jesus and Jesus alone to take me to heaven when I die
Thank you Lord Jesus for saving my soul............***Amen.***

If you just prayed this prayer and sent it from the bottom of your heart to the heart of God, then you have become a member of the family of God. Welcome to the Family!

This is Salvation and so many wonderful things have just taken place.
The angels in heaven are rejoicing and giving you a standing ovation. Your name has been written into the Lamb's Book of Life. You have been indwelled by the Holy Spirit never to be forsaken. Your salvation is signed, sealed and delivered. Nothing can separate you from the love of God. He will never forsake you and He will never leave you. You are now a child of God. You are a part of the family of God. You have an inheritance with the Son. You are joint heirs with Christ. You will someday see Jesus face to face and He will walk with you in the City of God. You will walk streets of gold and breathe celestial air. Your spirit has been regenerated; brought back to life; born again. You can openly communicate with the living God through prayer and Scripture. You will now be able to read His Word with understanding and God will speak to your heart. He knows you. He loves you and He wants to fellowship with you.

I could go on and on about the great things that God has in store for you but your greatest need right now is to get together with other born again Bible believing Christians. Find a good Bible Church and become faithful. The Lord wants to help you to become the kind of person that down deep inside you always wanted to become and He wants you to grow spiritually and to walk in the Word. I would encourage you to get an Authorized King James Bible and read it; a good one is the Cambridge Bible. A good place to start is with the Gospel of John.

We live in exciting times. We are living in the 'Church Age' and in fact I believe that we are now living at the very end of the 'Church Age'. I believe that within our life time the sky is going to split wide open, the trumpet shall sound, Jesus will descend and we shall be caught up to be with Him in the air. You will now be a part of this and He wants you there!

1 Thessalonians 4:16-17
16. For the Lord himself shall descend from heaven with a shout, with the voice of the archangel, and with the trump of God: and the dead in Christ shall rise first:
17. Then we which are alive *and* remain shall be caught up together with them in the clouds, to meet the Lord in the air: and so shall we ever be with the Lord.

I pray that God will Bless your life and make your life a Blessing to others.

Chapter Eight

IN CLOSING

This book was several years in the making. I was completely taken back by the amount of information available on the Authorized King James Bible and the many modern day Bibles that are in the market today. It is overwhelming. The Internet proved to be information overload. It was like trying to run through waist deep water while dragging an anchor. I read through many books, some of them several times, along with article after article both pro and con until I thought my mind was going to explode. I watched movies and videos, and listened to a countless number of sermons. About a year into this study the lights came on and I came to the conclusion that the Authorized King James Bible is in fact the Real Deal.

I was so excited. The more I learned, the more I wanted to share this information with everyone. I have been saved for over forty years and during this time I have often been asked to preach or teach. I have run a Junior Church, taught Sunday school classes for the teens, adults and even an adult handicapped class. I taught a science course at a Christian Home School, worked on a Bus Ministry, started a Men's fastball team called Maranatha and handed out Gospel tracks to the opposition players. I have gone door to door soul winning, done some street preaching, filled in the pulpit many

times when Preachers were away, preached several funerals, preached for a Hospital visitation program and the Awana program and have given my testimony at several churches and Christian functions and organizations and even took a Home Bible Institute course. I have been through some very good times, some true mountain top experiences and made it through some very difficult down in the valley situations as well.
Hind-site being 20:20 it was all good.

Romans 8:28
And we know that all things work together for good to them that love God, to them who are the called according to *his* purpose.

As I mentioned before, I am very 'Old School' when it comes to my Biblical Positions. Some of my heroes were men like Lester Rolof, Jack Hyles, John R. Rice, Robert G. Lee, J Vernon McGee, Oliver Green, Oswald J. Smith, Perry F. Rockwood, Les Campbell and many other great preachers and evangelists. I cut my spiritual teeth on King James Bible preaching; sermons like Pawing in the Valley, Fresh Oil and Pay Day Someday. As a very young Christian, I was graciously delivered from the Charismatic Movement by a John R. Rice book on Tongues. I was fortunate to get saved under Pastor Craig who was perhaps the greatest preacher and teacher I ever had. He spent hours with me as a young Christian. He was not just a great preacher but a great pastor, a mentor who gave himself to his people and because of my stubborn self will we broke fellowship and I went to another Church. Sometimes Christians can be so stupid and this was one of those times in my life. He gave me a great foundation and I credit his teaching for the fact that I am still walking with the Lord today. He taught me to be ready to preach or die at a moment's notice. He taught me to give until it hurts and then to keep giving until it stops hurting. He is a big part of any success that I have enjoyed as a Christian and I remain in his debt.

I have never attended a Church that did not preach from the Authorized King James Bible. Because of this, I thought that I could take the information that I had put together and use it to encourage the Church family. Seriously, I thought this was good stuff and I wanted to share it with everyone. You see, that is how I am. When I learn something new, I love to open the Bible and teach it. I thought for sure, that the information on the King James Bible would be openly accepted and appreciated, especially since this Church has never had a Preacher or a Sunday School teacher (to my knowledge) that has ever used anything but the King James Bible.

Well, as it turned out, it didn't quite work that way. I was surprised and a bit confused by some of the reaction I stirred up. I was only aware of two or three people in our Church that read from one of the new modern day Bibles and there was never any animosity directed towards me that I was aware of. I considered these people to be my friends and I still do.

One of my personal friends reads from the NIV. I am not sure what his wife reads from, but it has never come up in our conversations and it has never been a problem with our fellowship. We have been in their home for dinner and barbeques and they have been at our home many times. We have hunted and fished together and even travelled together on vacations. We are and remain good friends. In fact their son, who is a walking Biblical Library and borderline genius, sent me some literature and videos that were very helpful in my studies.

Whenever I preach or teach, I try to encourage people in their walk with the Lord and I have never had any one particular person in my cross-hairs. I have been around long enough to see the pulpit used this way and each time it was heart breaking, especially for the person to whom it was directed. When I make a point in scripture, I want people to know that the point is based on the solid foundation of God's inspired and inerrant Word.

No one has ever said anything directly to me about being offended with my stance on the KJV Bible, but as most of you know, once you let the dog off the chain it often runs wild. I had no idea how divisive my position on the Authorized King James Bible being a copy of the Inspired and Preserved Word of God was going to be, however, I soon got the message, loud and clear and oh yes, the dog was definitely off the chain! To say that I had the wind taken out of my sails is an understatement. This was disturbing and very difficult for me to understand. Those who know me best, know that I have a very compassionate heart and care very deeply about people and often go out of my way to meet other people's needs.

There is a lot of miss-information today concerning the King James Only Movement. Many good Bible believing people who hold to the KJV as their Bible of choice have been labeled as such. In the process of this study, I have read many articles on the King James Only Movement; such as Peter Ruckman chalk videos; sermon videos; and many other articles concerning this movement. Peter Ruckman is a bit rough around the edges and a bit crude in his defense of the King James Bible but most of the attacks on him were personal in nature with very little substantive argument concerning his Biblical position on the KJV. That is exactly what the liberal Evangelical camp manages to do so well; they attack the character instead of the issue.

Even though I hold very strongly to the Authorized King James Bible, I do not believe that I fall into the camp of the King James Only Movement.

A lot of the people who attack the King James Bible are intellectual unbelieving secular humanists who not only want to destroy the Bible, but also want to destroy any Christian influence within our society, our schools, our governments, our courts and our Christian Holidays; Easter and Christmas. I was watching a late night talk show on TV and they had as their guest one of the lead actors from the TV program *M.A.S.H*. He was asked what he thought was the problem with the world today and he blurted out "The King James Bible" and went off on a rant that was rather chilling. His rant was not surprising when you think of how Hollywood has treated Christianity in many movies and TV programs and his tirade fell in line with the mindset of the uneducated majority when it comes to the Word of God.

However, some of the men who attack the King James Bible are good Christian men and this for me is perhaps the cruelest blow of all. (*Et tu, Brute*) I honestly believe that most of them have never really studied or investigated this issue at any length and have blindly lined themselves up with someone else's opinion. However, some of them went to Seminaries that had curriculums that degraded the Textus Receptus and have fallen victim to the Westcott and Hort position or philosophy as I prefer to call it. Many of the articles from these preachers concerning the King James Only Movement are very condescending, visceral and mean spirited. In fact they can be as mean spirited as some of the King James Only crowd can be with their literature and videos.

Many of the critics are Preachers who are into writing a lot of Christian literature; books on Christian living, reference Bibles, Bible studies, Commentaries and several books a year to help support their ministry. For many of them it is all about the money. Many of the people who buy their books are into the 'new' Bibles and they do not want to offend and thus hurt their sales. Most of their literature and books no longer have the KJV version when they quote scripture. In fact you can go through an entire Bible study and not have any verses in the KJV; sad but true. I challenge you to check out the many TV ministries that are into selling a new book every month and check out their Bible of choice. In most cases you will find

In Closing

it is the NKJV or the NASB or the ESV or a combination of the many new Bibles in the market.

When was the last time you went into a Bible Book Store in search of an Authorized King James Bible? Try it sometime and tell me what you find.......everything but a King James Bible. In fact go to the Book Store on most of the Christian Universities and Colleges and see if you can find one.

I believe that secular humanism is largely responsible for the kind of textual criticism that ushered in the flood of new Bibles on the market. I also believe the modern day Bibles who have their foundation in the Alexandrian Stream of Bibles are causing serious confusion within the Church when they take away from and add to the Scriptures. When people cut words and verses out of a copy of the Original Inspired Word of God and/or add words that were never in or a part of the Original Inspired Word and thus change the intended meaning of a verse or a chapter, then I call this corrupting the Word of God.

Jeremiah 23:36
And the burden of the LORD shall ye mention no more: for every man's word shall be his burden; for ye have perverted the words of the living God, of the LORD of hosts our God.

1 Corinthians 14:33
For God is not *the author* of confusion, but of peace, as in all churches of the saints.

I am going to go a bit off topic for a minute to deal with a problem that I see within the Church. When I was first saved back in the 70's, being an Independent Fundamental Baptist was considered a good thing. A Fundamental Baptist Church was one that read and taught from the Authorized King James Bible and had Standards for Christian Service based on the Bible i.e. for a Deacon, for a Sunday school teacher, an Assistant Pastor, a Youth Pastor etc. We were supposed to be people with Biblical convictions; people who lived by Biblical principles. Back in the day, obedience to the Word was how a Christian was measured. We were expected to set a good example and have enough spiritual depth and maturity to disciple the younger Christian.

When I was first saved, not only did my Preacher spend some quality time with me, but the man who lead me to the Lord invited my wife and I into their home on many occasions and we became the best of friends. A Deacon in the Church also invited my wife and I into his home to fellowship and encouraged us in the Lord and we became the best of friends. The Adult Sunday school teacher also had us over to his home and we became the best of friends.

Do you see a pattern here? My wife and I were in constant fellowship and we were greatly encouraged in our walk with the Lord. With the great preaching from the pulpit, the teaching from my Sunday school teacher and reading my Bible every day, I grew in the Lord.

Very soon into our salvation, the Pastor spoke to us about believer's baptism and Lynda and I got baptized. A few months later the Pastor asked me to go with him on some visitations. He did the talking and I did the listening and only spoke when asked. To be honest with you, I was too intimidated to say anything but slowly I grew and the Lord started to use me. Then the Pastor asked me to take him to visit some of my friends. This is where the tire hit the road; talk about intimidating. Then the Pastor asked me to give my testimony in Church and to invite my family. I was terrified to get up in front of people but the Lord saw me through it and I continued to grow in the Lord. I gave my testimony in many other Churches and Christian functions and continued to be faithful in Sunday School and Church and to read and study the Bible every day. Many times I would stop by the Church and ask my Pastor question after question and continued to grow to the point that he asked me to help out with a Bus Ministry and to run a junior church with the bus kids. This is what I would call true discipleship. My Pastor worked with me over a long period of time and helped me to get to a point where I was ready for Christian service.

True discipleship is what separated the Fundamental Church from the Evangelical Church. The Evangelical Movement is all inclusive; no repentance; no standards; no convictions; rock music; very little structure; wide open to the Charismatic Movement; rejection of the King James Bible and a just as you are; stay as you are; God is good; He loves me; He loves you; we are all ok type of messages!

Today, being a Fundamentalist Church is considered a bad thing. We are accused of being hard hearted legalists, only looking at the outward appearance of man and having no compassion and love for the sinner. I like what my current Pastor has to say about sinners; win them where they are and love them to where they need to be. Winning the lost and discipleship should be synonymous. However, in many cases we win a person to Christ and before they ever attend Sunday school and/or Church on a regular basis and get grounded in the Word, they are allowed to get actively involved in one of the ministries. Many Churches have a full array of ministries; Nursery, Sunday School for all ages, Awana, Junior Church, Choir, Film Ministries, Bus Ministries, Youth Groups, Teenage Groups, Young Married Groups, Vacation Bible Schools etc. Unfortunately, in many cases, there are just not enough qualified people to staff them properly. Often a young Christian in their enthusiasm will offer to help and because we are desperately in need of help, we let it happen. This is like giving the keys of the car to a twelve year old in a snow storm and then wonder what happened when he or she goes off the road and into the ditch. Babes in Christ still in need of the sincere milk of the Word, no spiritual depth, no understanding of basic Christian principals, no root, no maturity and before you know it they get offended and are gone. Allowing this to happen is not loving them to where they need to be. This is compromise and it is dangerous because Satan uses these kind of situations to discourage and frustrate the new believer.

We need to get some real discipleship Sunday School programs going that are temporary and set up for new believers only. We need to teach them the basics and give them a sound foundation for their spiritual growth. Once we have covered the basics, then we need to move them into a regular Sunday School class where they can get into the meat of the Word with mature Christians who will love them to where they need to be and help prepare them to effectively take part in Christian service. Teach them; love them; train them; love them; use them; love them!

Now back to the objective of this book; the Bible, the Word of God.

Here is the problem as I understand it and as I experienced it. It was largely through the Evangelical Movement that the Modern Day Bibles became popular. The Evangelical Churches and Ministries actively pushed these modern day Bibles on their congregations from the pulpit and through their Christian literature, books and seminars. The Evangelicals write more books and literature than the Fundamentalists ever thought of. In many cases they are the over educated, professional student, type person who considers themself as the authoritative intellectual on all spiritual matters.

The first year I was saved, I attended a Family Life Seminar in Buffalo NY where they actively and aggressively promoted the NASB as being the best thing since sliced bread. I was a relatively new Christian and got talked into purchasing an NASB New Testament. I found myself trying to cross reference the NASB with my KJV only to get confused and frustrated. Within a few months I discarded the

NASB and went back to my KJV. The NASB did not speak to my heart like my KJV Bible and now I understand why.

Today, many of the people who are actively reading these 'new' modern day Bibles are High School and College age young people; good young people who love the Lord, but good young people who have never read the KJV. They have been taught that the King James Bible is out dated, too hard to understand and that the new Bibles have been translated from documents that are more accurate than the manuscripts used to translate the Authorized King James Bible. Because of these false teachings and accusations, they are now reading from Bibles that have changed the Inspired Word of God. In their young minds the absolutes of God's Word have been put into question. They are being taught the Doctrine of Limited Inspiration i.e. only the Original Documents were inspired and with the changing (perverting) of ***Psalm 12:7*** in these new Bibles, they are not being taught the Doctrine of the Preservation of God's Word.

Not only is the Foundation of their Faith being attacked by the humanistic secular public school systems, the attack is also coming from the class rooms of many of the Evangelical Christian schools. However, what upsets me the most is that the attack is now coming from the pulpits and schools that were once sound KJV Fundamental institutions. Our young people are being bombarded with questions.......... "Is the Bible really the Inspired Word of God?" "Can we trust it?" "Do we have a copy of the Inspired Word of God available today?" "Did the Lord Preserve the pure words of God or is the Bible '*Just Another Book*' from antiquity written by fallible man and therefore corrupted over time and subject to error?" "Is the story of creation fact or allegory?" "Were Adam and Eve real people?" "Is the story of Jonah fact or metaphor?" "Do you really believe that a virgin can have a baby?" "Is the virgin birth a necessary part of God's Plan of Salvation?"

Can you hear him? Listen carefully. It's just a whisper....... *Yea hath God said?*
Many young people go to secular schools where they teach Evolution as fact and are hostile to any students who dare take a stand for Creation or the new buzz words Intelligent Design. The next thing that happens is a slick teacher enters the picture and unravels their faith; suddenly it is the Big Bang Theory and Evolution.

For myself it started in Grade 10 with an English teacher who taught 'fatalism'; then Grade 12 with a Science and a Biology teacher with the Big Bang and the Theory of Evolution; then my first year of University with a Philosophy 101 teacher who taught that God is just a figment of man's imagination! If you expressed the fact that you believed in God and in Divine Creation you were made to look foolish or naïve in front of the whole class.

Many Christian Schools today no longer hold to the Genesis account of Creation; they teach some form of Theistic Evolution and/or the Gap Theory and bring into question the Biblical and Historical truth of the Book of Genesis. This is a direct by-product of the modern day Evangelical movement and their Bibles that have flooded our Churches today.

I often feel caught between a rock and a hard place over these issues and I am not sure what I can do to turn this around other than writing this book. Without the reading of the true and preserved Word of God how can Biblical Faith prevail?

Luke 18:8 ....Nevertheless when the Son of man cometh, shall he find faith on the earth?

Today we live in the World of Political Correctness. Political Correctness comes straight from Satan himself. Satan is the father of the Politically Correct movement. Because of this, wrong has become right and right has become wrong. Life as the Christian knows it, is under attack. You can no longer take a stand on such issues as same sex marriage or abortion unless you want to be classified as a homophobe or hating women. There is no such thing as sin and as a result there is a loss of respect for morality and the sanctity of life. Everything is governed by situation ethics and sin has become both irrelevant and unfashionable to preach on.

Proverbs 30:12
There is a generation *that are* pure in their own eyes, and *yet* is not washed from their filthiness.

Judges 17:6
In those days *there was* no king in Israel, *but* every man did *that which was* right in his own eyes.

    I graduated from the State University of New York at Buffalo. It was one of the most far left Universities going. When I look at the political landscape in the USA and Canada today, it is obvious that these far left radicals are now in control; they run our government, our public schools and our universities. They have a political agenda that is diabolically opposed to sound Biblical Principles. Today our political leaders and our teachers look us straight in the eye and lie without even a blink. Sadly, the same can be said for our Churches and Christianity today. The left wing, liberal minded politically correct Evangelicals are running the show. Their teachings and philosophies have permeated into the Fundamental Churches through their literature, their seminars, their videos and their Modern Day Bibles. We are no longer able to stand up to and/or criticize them on their positions, because that would be unkind and that would be unloving and that would be politically incorrect. Today if you believe that the King James Bible is an exact copy of the Divinely Inspired and Preserved Word of God, you are classified as King James Only, held in contempt and considered to be a politically incorrect heretic.

The Bible is God's Revelation of Himself to man. These Revelations were given to man in God's own timing, in God's own words and according to God's own mindset. That is what History is; His Story; and He told His Story in His own Words.

Isaiah 55:8–9
8. For my thoughts *are* not your thoughts, neither *are* your ways my ways, saith the LORD.
9. For *as* the heavens are higher than the earth, so are my ways higher than your ways, and my thoughts than your thoughts.

I am going to say something that may be a bit confusing, but bear with me and think it through. The Bible is God's Inspired Revelation of who He is, however, the language itself is not Inspired. It is the Message that God gave to man that is Inspired; His Message in His Words about Himself; His Message in His Words about Creation; His Message in His Words about the Flood; His Message in His Words about Salvation; His thoughts from His mindset.

God not only gave us this Inspired Revelation of Himself, He also promised to keep and protect His Words and His Message down through the ages through Divine Preservation. (Psalm 12: 6 -7 2Timothy.3:16)

I believe my Authorized King James Bible 1769 edition is Inspired, not because God inspired the 'Translators' or the 'English language'. My King James Bible is Inspired because it is an exact word for word translation of the 'Preserved Copies' of the 'Original Inspired Word of God' into the English language and it is therefore without error and perfect.

**If this position makes me King James Only
then I am guilty as charged.**

In Closing

Let me say something about those who read from one of the modern day Bibles. I have heard some awesome preaching from Preachers who use another Bible; men like John Piper, Alistair Begg, Charles Price, David Jeremiah etc. These are men who I believe spend time on their knees preparing their messages and then deliver them with great authority, power and passion. Men that I respect, but men that I do not necessarily agree with on some of their Biblical positions and doctrine. Never the less, God has used them to speak to my heart. What humors me a bit is that many of these men, when they are in the middle of a message and quote some scripture off the top of their head, it often comes out in the King James Bible verse. Many of these men who are now preaching from one of these modern day Bibles actually got saved under the preaching and teaching of the King James Bible; after all it has been the Bible of choice for over 400 years in most of the main line Protestant Churches. In fact, it was the King James Bible in 1611 that separated the Protestant Church from the Church at Rome and still does to this day.

I recently went to an outstanding ministry in Kentucky. Many of you will know who I am talking about just by mentioning the name of the State. Their entire ministry is predicated on the Book of Genesis being the inspired, inerrant Word of God. They take the position that the Bible is to be accepted as the literal, plenary, inspired Word of God and is therefore perfect and without error. It is a truly amazing ministry and I purchased several series of their tapes and took out a three year subscription of their quarterly magazine and plan on ordering this magazine for my sons. This ministry has a major concern about the fact that we are losing our youth and have stated the need for apologetic type teaching designed to equip our young people with the Biblical knowledge that they need to defend themselves against the spiritual attacks on their faith in the school systems. This kind of ministry is absolutely critical for our young people today and I mean absolutely critical! Seriously, I was pumped!

Having said this, you have no idea how discouraged and disappointed I was to see the leader of this ministry reading and teaching from the NASB and the NKJV in his videos? The NASB and the NKJV are not the Bible that a ministry of this importance and magnitude should be using. The NASB and the NKJV are just one of the many modern day Bibles that are causing confusion and doubt within the family of God. The NASB and the NKJV have so many changes in the text and so many confusing marginal notes that it boggles my mind that such a great ministry would lean so heavily on them. How confusing it must be for young people who read a verse and then go to the marginal note where it says something like 'many mss. do not contain this verse, or 'not found in most of the old mss.' etc. What does a Bible like this do for young people that are already under attack from their education system and are looking for some absolutes to hold on to?

The writers of the NASB and the NKJV believed in the Inspiration of the Original Documents only and do not hold to the doctrine of Divine Preservation. In one of the video's he makes the point that the words of the Lord are pure words and using the NASB he shows the first few words in Psalm 12: 6. But what he did not show was the entire teaching on this subject as presented in *Psalm 12: 6–7*. These two verses go together and to separate or change these two verses would take away from the truth concerning the Doctrines of Inspiration and Preservation.

<u>*Let's look at and compare Psalm 12: 6-7.*</u>
Psalm 12: 6–7 <u>KJV</u>

6. The words of the LORD *are* pure words: *as* silver tried in a furnace of earth, purified seven times.

7. Thou shalt keep them, O LORD, thou shalt preserve them from this generation for ever.

Psalm 12: 6–7 NASB
6. The words of the Lord are pure words; As silver tried in a furnace on the earth, refined seven times.
7. You, O Lord, will keep them; You will preserve him from this generation forever.

Now you tell me, where does the NASB stand on the Preservation of God's Word?
The NASB rendering of Psalm 12: 7 does not even make sense when you look at it.
………..you will preserve '*him*'…… who or what is '*him*' referring to?
The following two verses are an incorrect rendering of God's Word as well.
(DRB) (12:8) Thou, O Lord, wilt preserve us: and keep us from this generation for ever.
(ESV) You, O LORD, will keep them; you will guard us from this generation forever.
The KJV has this verse correct. It is the pure words of the Lord that are being kept and preserved. For once the NKJV agrees with the KJV and has these verses correct and with no confusing foot notes; imagine that!
One of my hero's when I was first saved was a man named Dr. Henry M. Morris, a founding father of the Institute for Creation Research USA. This man went where angles feared to tread. He ventured on to the campuses of the major liberal Universities in the USA and Canada and openly debated the best Science Professors that these universities had to offer. Dr. Morris literally wiped the floor with them. Eventually, his opportunities to debate these great scientific minds dried up as the Universities sent out warnings not to invite this man on campus. Dr. Morris also took a strong stand against the liberal mindset of men like Rudolf Kittel and Westcott and Hort, as he exposed them for their rejection of Biblical inerrancy and how they were devoted to evolutionism. In an

article that I read on line from, Bible Versions, section 11. Modern Versions & Translators, there was a quote from the late Dr. Morris.

Dr. Morris issued this statement concerning the Bible; *"I believe therefore, after studying, teaching and loving the Bible for over 55 years, that Christians; especially creationists; need to hang on to their old King James Bibles as long as they live. God has uniquely blessed its use in the great revivals, in the world-wide missionary movement and in the personal lives of believers, more so than He has with all the rest of the versions put together, and 'by their fruits ye shall know them ' (Matthew 7:20). It is the most beautiful, most powerful and (I strongly believe), the most reliable of any that we have or ever will have, until Christ returns."*

What a powerful statement from such a great man of God in the Creation Movement. What a shame that the current leaders in this wonderful ministry in Kentucky do not embrace the position of one of the leading founders of Creation Research.

Having said this, I have no intention of throwing this amazing ministry from the great State of Kentucky under the bus. I will continue to subscribe to their quarterly magazine and will also continue to encourage other Christians to visit them. This is a great ministry, one that every Church should take their teenagers to visit and one that I will continue to support and look forward to visiting again.

Their greatest concern is the attack that the world has launched against the Foundations of the Word of God and yet they read and teach from Bibles that do just that? How much more effective this ministry could be if they used the Bible that God has blessed for over 400 years and which many of the world's leading Missionaries carried into every nock and cranny of the known world and from which many of the world's greatest Preachers and Evangelists thundered forth God's Plan of Salvation and Redemption. Instead they

In Closing

have lined themselves up with versions that are part of the Second Stream of Bibles, who's Old Testament, upon which they predicate their entire ministry, is based on the corrupt Ben Asher Leningrad Manuscript and/or the Septuagint. Seriously, I just don't get it?

Allow me to make another important point. Just because a person reads from the King James Bible does not necessarily prevent them from going off into a cult. One of the better books that I read on the King James Bible is 'Our Authorized Bible Vindicated'. It was written by Benjamin G. Wilkinson (1872-1968) a Seventh Day Adventist; a Mormon!

A cult is the result of a person or a group that deliberately takes portions of scripture and reduces them to metaphors and allegory and twist God's Word to fit into some man-made misplaced and unbiblical theology. That is why most cults will require their followers to read other books and literature that go directly against the Bible and/or like the Jehovah Witness they will revise the Bible and change it to fit into their own theology. The Jehovah Witness insist that their followers read not only their Bible but also the "Watch Tower" magazine. The Mormons believe that the Inspiration of Scripture continued with their modern day apostles and prophets like Joseph Smith and insist that their followers read and study the "Book of Mormon" which they accept as Holy Scripture as well. They therefore have to take a position that discredits the inerrancy and infallibility of the Authorized King James Bible claiming that it has many errors and contradictions. When Benjamin Wilkinson published his book 'Our Authorized Bible Vindicated' it was not well received within the Mormon community and many of his college colleagues and professors openly criticized him and rejected his book publicly.

Although I did not detect any Mormon theology coming through in Wilkinson's book, we must always guard ourselves against the wiles of the Devil and even though Benjamin

Wilkinson wrote a good book on the King James Bible, he unfortunately never indicated that he was saved by grace and his faith was not placed into the Biblical Jesus that we know and love.

We have to understand that many of the cults are well versed in their theology and doctrines and are well prepared to challenge your Christian faith in Jesus Christ. If you are going to do a spiritual sword drill with a Jehovah's Witness or a Mormon, you better have a good grip on the Word of God. Many of them are trained and well prepared with a whole list of scripture verses that they will use against you....... yea hath God said! If you are confronted and find yourself intimidated by these people, then the best thing you can do is not to argue with them over scripture. Give your testimony on how you got saved and in the process give them God's plan of Salvation and tell them how much you love the Lord Jesus Christ. Your testimony is powerful and God can use it!

Galatians 3:1
O foolish Galatians, who hath bewitched you, that ye should not obey the truth, before whose eyes Jesus Christ hath been evidently set forth, crucified among you?

If a person truly believes and has put their faith into who Jesus is......God the Son...the second person in the Trinity.....His virgin birth and that Jesus is God in the flesh.... the Son of God .....His sinless life....The shedding of His Blood through His death on the Cross....His burial and His resurrection.....that God has physically raised Him from the dead......and admits that they are a sinner in need of a saviour..... and with a repentant heart asks for forgiveness of his sins....and calls on the name of the Lord.....inviting Jesus Christ into their heart as their personal Lord and Saviour....... then I don't care if they read from the M I C K E Y (mouse) Bible, they are saved and a part of the family of God and are

In Closing

therefore my Brother and my Sister in the Lord and I will do everything I can to encourage them in their Christian walk.
Whew! Did you get all that?

1 John 4:10–11
10. Herein is love, not that we loved God, but that he loved us, and sent his Son *to be* the propitiation for our sins.
11. Beloved, if God so loved us, we ought also to love one another.

If my friends and my family were honest, they would tell you that they used to read from the Authorized King James Bible and in fact if they were totally honest they would tell you that they got saved under the preaching and the teaching from the Authorized King James Bible. But now, for some reason it is too hard to understand; go figure?

If you want a Bible that God has truly blessed, then it would be the Authorized King James Bible. The King James Bible stands alone amongst all of the modern day English Bibles. If you happen to be one of those people who have put your King James Bible on the shelf then I encourage you to pick it back up and allow it to speak to your heart once again. If you have never owned a King James Bible then purchase one. It will be the best investment you ever make. A good edition is the Cambridge, Red Letter Edition. It has the Translator's letter to King James as well as their letter to the Reader, both of which are a must read.

Reference Books on the King James Bible:
The following books are excellent reading on the subject of the Bible. I recommend these books to anyone who wants a better understanding concerning your Bible of choice.

1. "Final Authority" – A Christian's Guide to the King James Bible by William P. Grady

2. "One Book Stands Alone" – The Key to Understanding the Bible by Dr. Douglas Stauffer
3. "Which Bible?" – Edited by David Otis Fuller
4. "The King James Version Defended" by Edward F. Hills
5. "Our Authorized Bible Vindicated" by Benjamin G. Wilkinson (Mormon Missionary)
6. "The Men Behind the King James Version" by Gustavus Paine
7. "Translator's Revised" by Alexander McClure
8. "Let's Weigh the Evidence" by Barry D. Burton (good one for teens and new Christians)
9. "And These Three are One" – an Exegesis by Jesse M. Boyd, Wake Forest N.C.

These are just the tip of the iceberg. There are many other excellent books, articles, video's and messages on the King James Bible, however, these are a good start if you want to begin your own personal journey to understanding the 'Truth' and to understand just how our Heavenly Father provided a copy of the Inspired and Inerrant Word of God for us today. There are many websites such as the 'Dean Burgon Society', 'Bible Versions' etc. that have a wealth of information on the subject of the Bible and are well worth your time to investigate.

Proverbs 22: 17–21
17. Bow down thine ear, and hear the words of the wise, and apply thine heart unto my knowledge.
18. For *it is* a pleasant thing if thou keep them within thee; they shall withal be fitted in thy lips.
19. That thy trust may be in the LORD, I have made known to thee this day, even to thee.
20. Have not I written to thee excellent things in counsels and knowledge,

21. That I might make thee know the certainty of the words of truth; that thou mightest answer the words of truth to them that send unto thee?

In the past I have vigorously defended the King James Bible and will continue to do so when required. However, as a result of my research on the Bible, I have come to the conclusion that in reality, the Authorized King James Bible needs no defending.

The Authorized King James Bible is like a pit bull on a chain. All we have to do is turn it loose and it will defend itself.

Just Grip it and Rip it!

May God Bless You and Make You a Blessing!
Michael Dunn

1 Peter 1:22 - 23
Maranatha – The Lord is Coming!